The Spokesman
The Third Way
to the Servile State

AF192473

Edited by Ken Coates
Published by Spokesman for the
Bertrand Russell Peace Foundation

Spokesman 66   1999

CONTENTS

Subscriptions
Institutions £30.00
Individuals £20.00

Back issues available on
request

A CIP catalogue record
for this book is available
from the British Library

Published by the
Bertrand Russell Peace
Foundation Ltd.,
Russell House
Bulwell Lane
Nottingham NG6 0BT
England
Tel. 0115 9784504
email:
elfeuro@compuserve.com

Printed by the Russell Press Ltd., Nottingham, UK

ISSN 0262 7922   ISBN 0 85124 626 5

Editorial

The **Spokesman** has taken a very keen interest in the problem of unemployment in Europe, and has, in addition to publishing a string of books on the question, also published all the papers of the founding Convention of the Campaign for Full Employment. This Convention drew together representatives of many different political Parties and Churches, but it was most notable for the fact that it also attracted representation from all the active pressure groups which are organising or working for the unemployed throughout Europe.

The first Convention drew almost a thousand participants, from every country in the European Union, and some outside. The second Convention encountered some organisational difficulties because of changes in the availability of some of the facilities in the European Parliament. Even so, more than six hundred people participated, and maintained a very high level of discussion in all the workshops that were organised.

There is strong demand from these participants that a further Convention be organised, because there are no equivalent possibilities open to the unemployed to register an impact on the political process, at the same time as networking to defend their own interests.

But the political framework has been changing remorselessly, and although the second Convention was only held in February 1999, there are already very strong pressures for changes in official policy which, if they proved successful, would be likely to cause a significant further deterioration in the condition of the unemployed, and in the continuing security of those who remain at work.

Early this year, British Prime Minister Blair met with Spanish Premier Aznar to launch a Joint Declaration on these issues. It called for an agreement to revise the employment policies of the European Union, prioritising de-regulation. Specifically, it proposed that a new policy be agreed, in time to be launched at the Lisbon Summit in March 2000.

Hot on the heels of the Blair/Aznar Declaration, came another joint declaration by the British Prime Minister and Chancellor Schroeder in Germany. This celebrated the Third Way without specifying any destination. To it we devote a large part of the present number of the **Spokesman**.

Schroeder's decision to embrace the Third Way has caused consternation in Germany, especially among the trade unions, Churches, and those parts of public opinion which have always affirmed social solidarity as the cornerstone of postwar German democracy.

To make no bones about it, the Third Way is a full-scale neo-liberal offensive, crafted in accordance with the social philosophy of Mrs. Thatcher. In Germany, the attempt to push forward Blair/Thatcher policies has met with a powerful opposing reaction. The governing Parties have lost heavily in regional elections. In the East, the SPD now polls lower votes than the PDS, the new Left Party which emerged, first of all in the East, after the fall of the German Democratic Republic.

A major casualty of the Third Way was Oskar Lafontaine, a lifelong peace campaigner, who had embraced the cause of full employment, and in so doing became the champion of an alternative Europe. Lafontaine's forced resignation from the Government registered a powerful protest against neo-liberal policy on the one side, and the war against Yugoslavia on the other. In fact, the Third Way, and the policy of so-called ethical imperialism, are two sides of the same coin. Only on the basis of rigorous criticism of neo-liberalism and new imperialism will truly humanistic politics re-emerge.

Ken Coates

East Timor Is Not Yesterday's Story

Noam Chomsky

Noam Chomsky is Professor of Linguistics at the Massachusetts Institute of Technology. His latest book, The New Military Humanism: Lessons from Kosovo, *has just been published by Pluto Press, price £9.99. These articles first appeared on the ZNet website (www.znet.org).*

According to recent reports, the UN mission in East Timor (UNAMET) has been able to account for just over 150,000 people out of an estimated population of 850,000. It reports that 260,000 'are now languishing in squalid refugee camps in West Timor under the effective control of the militias after either fleeing or being forcibly removed from their homes', and that another 100,000 have been relocated to other parts of Indonesia. The rest are presumed to be hiding in the mountains. The Australian commander expressed the natural concern that displaced people lack food and medical supplies. Touring camps in East and West Timor, US Assistant Secretary of State Harold Koh reported that the refugees are 'starving and terrorized', and that disappearances 'without explanation' are a daily occurrence.

To appreciate the scale of this disaster, one has to bear in mind the virtual demolition of the physical basis for survival by the departing Indonesian army and its paramilitary associates ('militias'), and the reign of terror to which the territory has been subjected for a quarter-century, including the slaughter of hundreds of thousands of people when the Carter Administration was providing the required diplomatic and military support.

How have its successors reacted during the current 'noble phase' of foreign policy, with its 'saintly glow', to quote some of the awed rhetoric of respected commentators in the national press through the 1990s? One way was to increase the support for the killers – for 'our kind of guy', as General Suharto was described by the Clinton Administration before he fell from grace by losing control and failing to implement harsh IMF orders with sufficient ardour. After the 1991 Dili massacre, Congress restricted arms sales and banned US training of the Indonesian military, but Clinton found devious ways to evade the ban. Congress expressed its 'outrage', reiterating that 'it was and is the intent of Congress to prohibit US military training for Indonesia', as readers of the *Far Eastern Economic Review* and dissident publications here could learn. But to no avail.

Inquiries about Clinton's programmes received the routine response from the State Department: US military training 'serves a very positive function in terms of exposing foreign militaries to US values'. These values were exhibited as military aid to Indonesia flowed and government-licensed sales of armaments increased five-fold from fiscal 1997 to last year. A month ago (Sept. 19), the London *Observer* international news service and the *Guardian Weekly* published a story headlined 'US Trained Butchers of East Timor'. The report, by two respected correspondents, described Clinton's 'Iron Balance' programme, which trained Indonesian military in violation of congressional bans as late as 1998. Included were Kopassus units, the murderous forces that organized and directed the 'militias' and participated directly in their atrocities, as Washington was well aware – just as it knew that these long-time beneficiaries of US training were 'legendary for their cruelty' and in East Timor 'became the pioneer and exemplar for every kind of atrocity' (Ben Anderson, one of the world's leading Indonesia specialists).

Clinton's 'Iron Balance' programme provided these forces with more training in counterinsurgency and 'psychological operations', expertise that they put to use effectively at once. As they and their minions were burning down the capital city of Dili in September, murdering and rampaging, the Pentagon announced that 'A US-Indonesian training exercise focused on humanitarian and disaster relief activities concluded Aug. 25', five days before the referendum that elicited the sharp escalation in crimes – precisely as the political leadership in Washington expected, at least if they were reading their own intelligence reports.

All of this found its way to the memory hole that contains the past record of the crucial US support for the atrocities, granted the same (null) coverage as many other events of the past year; for example, the unanimous Senate vote on June 30th calling on the Clinton administration to link Indonesian military actions in East Timor to 'any loan or financial assistance to Indonesia', as readers could learn from the *Irish Times*.

For much of 1999, Western intellectuals have been engaged in one of history's most audacious displays of self-adulation over their magnificent performance in Kosovo. Among the many facets of this grand achievement dispatched to the proper place was the fact that the huge flow of brutalized refugees expelled after the bombing could receive little care, thanks to Washington's defunding of the responsible UN agency. Its staff was reduced 15% in 1998, and another 20% in January 1999; and it now endures the denunciations of the (also saintly) Tony Blair for its 'problematic performance' in the wake of the atrocities that were the anticipated consequence of US/UK bombing. While the mutual admiration society was performing as required, atrocities mounted in East Timor. Even prior to the August referendum, some 3-5000 had been killed according to credible Church sources, about twice the number killed prior to the bombing in Kosovo (with more than twice the population), according to NATO. As atrocities skyrocketed in September, Clinton watched silently, until compelled by domestic and international (mostly Australian) pressure to make at least some gestures. These were enough for the Indonesian Generals to reverse course at once, an indication of the latent power that has always been in reserve. A rational person can readily draw some conclusions about criminal culpability.

At last report, the US has provided no funds for the Australian-led UN intervention force (in contrast, Japan, long a fervent supporter of Indonesia, offered $100 million). But that is perhaps not surprising, in the light of its refusal to pay any of the costs of the UN civilian operations even in Kosovo. Washington has also asked the UN to reduce the scale of subsequent operations, because it might be called upon to pay some of the costs. Hundreds of thousands of missing people may be starving in the mountains, but the Air Force that excels in pinpoint destruction of civilian targets apparently lacks the capacity to airdrop food – and no call has been heard for even such an elementary humanitarian measure. Hundreds of thousands more are facing a grim fate within Indonesia. A word from Washington would suffice to end their torment, but there is no word, and no comment.

In Kosovo, preparation for war crimes trials has been underway since May, expedited at US-UK initiative, including unprecedented access to intelligence information. In East Timor, investigations are being discussed at leisure, with Indonesian participation and a tight deadline (Dec. 31). It is 'an absolute joke, a complete whitewash', according to UN officials quoted in the British press. A spokesperson for Amnesty International added that the inquiry as planned 'will cause East Timorese even more trauma than they have suffered already. It would be really insulting at this stage'. Indonesian Generals 'do not seem to be quaking in their boots', the Australian press reports. One reason is that 'some of the most damning evidence is likely to be . . . material plucked from the air waves by sophisticated US and Australian electronic intercept equipment', and the Generals feel confident that their old friends will not let them down – if only because the chain of responsibility might be hard to snap at just the right point.

There is also little effort to unearth evidence of atrocities in East Timor. In striking contrast, Kosovo has been swarming with police and medical forensic teams from the US and other countries in the hope of discovering large-scale atrocities that can be transmuted into justification for the NATO bombing of which they were the anticipated consequence – as Milosevic had planned all along, it is now claimed, though NATO Commander General Wesley Clark reported a month after the bombing that the alleged plans 'have never been shared with me' and that the NATO operation 'was not designed [by the political leadership] as a means of blocking Serb ethnic cleansing . . . There was never any intent to do that. That was not the idea'.

Commenting on Washington's refusal to lift a finger to help the victims of its crimes, the veteran Australian diplomat Richard Butler observed that 'it has been made very clear to me by senior American analysts that the facts of the alliance essentially are that: the US will respond proportionally, defined largely in terms of its own interests and threat assessment . . .' The remarks were not offered in criticism of Washington; rather, of his fellow Australians, who do not comprehend the facts of life: that others are to shoulder the burdens, and face the costs – which for Australia, may not be slight. It will hardly come as a great shock if a few years hence US corporations are cheerfully picking up the pieces in an Indonesia that resents Australian actions, but has few complaints about the overlord.

The chorus of self-adulation has subsided a bit, though not much. Far more important than these shameful performances is the failure to act – at once, and decisively – to save the remnants of one of the most terrible tragedies of this awful century.

*   *   *

Retrospective

It is not easy to write with feigned calm and dispassion about the events that have been unfolding in East Timor. Horror and shame are compounded by the fact that the crimes are so familiar and could so easily have been terminated. That has been true ever since Indonesia invaded in December 1975, relying on US diplomatic support and arms – used illegally, but with secret authorisation, even new arms shipments sent under the cover of an official 'embargo'. There has been no need to threaten bombing or even sanctions. It would have sufficed for the US and its allies to withdraw their active participation, and to inform their close associates in the Indonesian military command that the atrocities must be terminated and the territory granted the right of self-determination that has been upheld by the United Nations and the International Court of Justice. We cannot undo the past, but should at least be willing to recognise what we have done, and to face the moral responsibility of saving the remnants and providing ample reparations, a pathetic gesture of compensation for terrible crimes.

The latest chapter in this painful story of betrayal and complicity opened right after the referendum of Aug. 30, 1999, when the population voted overwhelmingly for independence. At once, atrocities mounted sharply, organised and directed by the Indonesian military (the TNI). The UN Mission in East Timor (UNAMET) gave its appraisal on September 11:

> The evidence for a direct link between the militia and the military is beyond any dispute and has been overwhelmingly documented by UNAMET over the last four months. But the scale and thoroughness of the destruction of East Timor in the past week has demonstrated a new level of open participation of the military in the implementation of what was previously a more veiled operation.

The Mission warned that 'the worst may be yet to come . . . It cannot be ruled out that these are the first stages of a genocidal campaign to stamp out the East Timorese problem by force'.

Indonesia historian John Roosa, an official observer of the vote, described the situation starkly: 'Given that the pogrom was so predictable, it was easily preventable . . . But in the weeks before the ballot, the Clinton Administration refused to discuss with Australia and other countries the formation of [an international force]. Even after the violence erupted, the Administration dithered for days', until compelled by international (primarily Australian) and domestic pressure to make some timid gestures.

The recent events will evoke bitter memories among those who do not prefer 'intentional ignorance'. We are witnessing a shameful replay of events of 20 years ago. After carrying out a huge slaughter in 1977-78 with the decisive support of the Carter Administration, Indonesia felt confident enough to permit a brief visit by members of the Jakarta diplomatic corps, among them US Ambassador Edward Masters. They recognised that an enormous humanitarian catastrophe had been created. The aftermath was described by Benedict Anderson, one of the most distinguished Indonesia scholars. 'For nine long months' of starvation and terror, Anderson testified at the United Nations, 'Ambassador Masters deliberately refrained, even within the walls of the State Department, from proposing humanitarian aid to East Timor', waiting 'until the generals in Jakarta gave him the green light' – until they felt 'secure enough to permit foreign visitors', as an internal State Department document recorded. Only then did Washington consider taking some steps to deal with the consequences of its actions.

As TNI forces and their paramilitaries were burning down the capital city of Dili in September 1999, murdering and rampaging with renewed intensity, the Pentagon announced, as we have seen, that 'A US-Indonesian training exercise focused on humanitarian and disaster relief activities concluded Aug. 25', five days before the referendum. The lessons were applied within days in the standard way, as all but the voluntarily blind must understand after many years of the same tales, the same outcomes.

One gruesome illustration was the coup that brought General Suharto to power in 1965. Army-led massacres slaughtered hundreds of thousands in a few months, mostly landless peasants, destroying the mass-based political party of the left, the PKI. The achievement elicited unrestrained euphoria in the West and fulsome praise for the Indonesian 'moderates', Suharto and his military accomplices, who had cleansed the society and opened it to foreign plunder. Secretary of Defence Robert McNamara informed Congress that US military aid and training had 'paid dividends' – including half a million corpses; 'enormous dividends', a congressional report concluded. McNamara informed President Johnson that that US military assistance 'encouraged [the army] to move against the PKI when the opportunity was presented'. Contacts with Indonesian military officers, including university programmes, were 'very significant factors in determining the favourable orientation of the new Indonesian political elite' (the army).

So matters have continued for 35 years of intensive military aid, training, and communication, up to the humanitarian training exercises of August 1999. A few months earlier, shortly after the massacre of dozens of refugees who had taken shelter in a Church in Liquica, Admiral Dennis Blair, US Pacific Commander, assured TNI commander General Wiranto of US support and assistance, proposing a new US training mission. In the face of this record, only briefly sampled, and duplicated repeatedly elsewhere, the government lauds 'the value of the years of training given to Indonesia's future military leaders in the United States and the millions of dollars in military aid for Indonesia', urging more of the same for Indonesia and throughout the world.

The reasons for the disgraceful record have sometimes been honestly recognised. During the latest phase of atrocities, a senior diplomat in Jakarta described 'the dilemma' faced by the great powers: 'Indonesia matters and East Timor doesn't'. It is therefore understandable that Washington should keep to ineffectual gestures of disapproval while insisting that internal security in East Timor 'is the responsibility of the Government of Indonesia, and we don't want to take that responsibility away from them' – the official stance a few days before the August referendum, repeated in full knowledge of how that 'responsibility' had been carried out, and maintained as the most dire predictions were quickly fulfilled.

The reasoning of the senior diplomat was spelled out more fully by two Asia specialists of the *New York Times*: the Clinton Administration, they write, 'has made the calculation that the United States must put its relationship with Indonesia, a mineral-rich nation of more than 200 million people, ahead of its concern over the political fate of East Timor, a tiny impoverished territory of 800,000 people that is seeking independence'. The second national journal quotes Douglas Paal, president of the Asia Pacific Policy Center, stating the facts of life: 'Timor is a speed bump on the road to dealing with Jakarta, and we've got to get over it safely. Indonesia is such a big place and so central to the stability of the region'.

The term 'stability' has long served as a code word, referring to a 'favourable orientation of the political elite' – favourable not to their populations, but to foreign investors and global managers.

In the rhetoric of official Washington, 'We don't have a dog running in the East Timor race'. Accordingly, what happens there is not our business. But after intensive Australian pressure, the calculations shifted: 'we have a very big dog running down there called Australia and we have to support it', a senior government official concluded. The survivors of US-backed crimes in a 'tiny impoverished territory' are not even a 'small dog'.

The guiding principles were well understood by those responsible for Indonesia's 1975 invasion. They were articulated by UN Ambassador Daniel Patrick Moynihan, in words that should be committed to memory by anyone with a serious interest in international affairs, human rights, and the rule of law. The Security Council condemned the invasion and ordered Indonesia to withdraw, but to no avail. In his 1978 memoirs, Moynihan explains why:

'The United States wished things to turn out as they did, and worked to bring this about. The Department of State desired that the United Nations prove utterly ineffective in whatever measures it undertook. This task was given to me, and I carried it forward with no inconsiderable success.'

Success was indeed considerable. Moynihan cites reports that within two months some 60,000 people had been killed, '10 percent of the population, almost the proportion of casualties experienced by the Soviet Union during the Second World War'. A sign of the success, he adds, is that within a year 'the subject disappeared from the press'. So it did, as the invaders intensified their assault. Atrocities peaked as Moynihan was writing in 1977-78. Relying on a new flow of advanced military equipment from the Human Rights Administration, the Indonesian military carried out a devastating attack against the hundreds of thousands who had fled to the mountains, driving the survivors to Indonesian control. It was then that highly credible Church sources in East Timor sought to make public the estimates of 200,000 deaths that came to be accepted years later, after constant denial. The US reaction to the carnage has already been described.

As the slaughter reached near-genocidal levels, Britain and France joined in, providing arms and diplomatic support. Other powers too sought to participate in the lucrative aggression and massacre, always following the principles that have been lucidly enunciated.

The story does not begin in 1975. East Timor had not been overlooked by the planners of the post-war world. The territory should be granted independence, Roosevelt's senior adviser Sumner Welles mused, but 'it would certainly take a thousand years'. With an awe-inspiring display of courage and fortitude, the people of East Timor have struggled to confound that cynical prediction, enduring monstrous disasters. Perhaps 50,000 lost their lives protecting a small contingent of Australian commandoes fighting the Japanese; their heroism may have saved Australia from Japanese invasion. A third of the population were victims of the first years of the 1975 Indonesian invasion, many more since.

The current year opened with a moment of hope. Indonesia's interim president Habibie called for a referendum with a choice between incorporation within Indonesia ('autonomy') or independence. The army moved at once to prevent this outcome by terror and intimidation. In the months leading to the August referendum, as we have seen, 3-5000 were killed according to highly credible Church sources – twice the number of deaths prior to the NATO bombing in Kosovo, more than four times the number relative to population. The terror was widespread and sadistic, intended as a warning of the fate awaiting those foolhardy enough to disregard the orders of the occupying army.

Braving violence and threats, almost the entire population voted, many emerging from hiding to do so. Close to 80% chose independence. Then followed the latest phase of TNI atrocities in an effort to reverse the outcome by slaughter and expulsion, while reducing much of the country to ashes. Within two weeks more than 10,000 might have been killed, according to Bishop Carlos

Filipe Belo, the Nobel Peace laureate who was driven from his country under a hail of bullets, his house burned down and the refugees sheltering there dispatched to an uncertain fate.

Even before Habibie's surprise call for a referendum, the army anticipated threats to its rule, including its control over East Timor's resources, and undertook careful planning with 'the aim, quite simply, . . . to destroy a nation'. The plans were known to Western intelligence, as has been the case from the outset. TNI recruited thousands of West Timorese and brought in forces from Java. More ominously, the military command sent units of its dread US-trained Kopassus special forces, and as senior military adviser, General Makarim, a US-trained intelligence specialist with experience in East Timor and 'a reputation for callous violence'.

Terror and destruction began early in the year. The TNI forces responsible have been described as 'rogue elements' in the West, a questionable judgement. There is good reason to accept Bishop Belo's assignment of direct responsibility to commanding General Wiranto in Jakarta. It appears that the militias have been managed by elite units of Kopassus, the 'crack special forces unit' that had 'been training regularly with US and Australian forces until their behaviour became too much of an embarrassment for their foreign friends', veteran Asia correspondent David Jenkins reports. These forces are 'legendary for their cruelty', Benedict Anderson observes: in East Timor they 'became the pioneer and exemplar for every kind of atrocity', including systematic rapes, tortures and executions, and organisation of hooded gangsters. They adopted the tactics of the US Phoenix programme in South Vietnam that killed tens of thousands of peasants and much of the indigenous South Vietnamese leadership, Jenkins writes, as well as 'the tactics employed by the Contras' in Nicaragua, following lessons taught by their CIA mentors. The state terrorists were 'not simply going after the most radical pro-independence people but going after the moderates, the people who have influence in their community'. 'It's Phoenix', a well-placed source in Jakarta reported: the aim is 'to terrorise everyone' – the NGOs, the Red Cross, the UN, the journalists.

Well before the referendum, the commander of the Indonesian military in Dili, Colonel Tono Suratman, warned of what was to come: 'I would like to convey the following', he said: 'if the pro-independents do win ... all will be destroyed... It will be worse than 23 years ago'. An army document of early May, when international agreement on the referendum was reached, ordered that 'Massacres should be carried out from village to village after the announcement of the ballot if the pro-independence supporters win'. The independence movement 'should be eliminated from its leadership down to its roots'. Citing diplomatic, church and militia sources, the Australian press reported 'that hundreds of modern assault rifles, grenades and mortars are being stockpiled, ready for use if the autonomy option is rejected at the ballot box'. It warned that the army-run militias might be planning a violent takeover of much of the territory if, despite the terror, the popular will would be expressed.

All of this was understood by the 'foreign friends', who also knew how to bring the terror to an end, but preferred evasive and ambiguous reactions that the Indonesian Generals could easily interpret as a 'green light' to carry out their work.

The sordid history must be viewed against the background of US-Indonesia relations in the post-war era. The rich resources of the archipelago, and its critical strategic location, guaranteed it the central role in US global planning. These factors lie behind US efforts 40 years ago to dismantle Indonesia, perceived as too independent and too democratic, even permitting participation of the leftist peasant-based PKI. The same factors account for Western support for the regime of killers and torturers who brought about a 'favourable orientation' in 1965. Their achievements were, furthermore, understood to be a vindication of Washington's wars in Indochina, motivated in large part by concerns that the 'virus' of independent nationalism might 'infect' Indonesia, to borrow Kissingerian rhetoric. Support for the invasion of East Timor and subsequent atrocities was reflexive, though a broader analysis should attend to the fact that the collapse of the Portuguese empire had much the same consequences in Africa, where South Africa was the agent of Western-backed terror. Throughout, Cold War pretexts were routinely invoked, serving as a convenient disguise for ugly motives and actions, particularly so in Southeast Asia.

Surely we should by now be willing to cast aside mythology and face the causes and consequences of our actions, not only in East Timor. In that tortured corner of the world there is still time, though very little time, to prevent a hideous consummation of one of the most appalling tragedies of the terrible century that is winding to a horrifying, wrenching close.

Eyewitness in East Timor

*Reflections of a
UN Volunteer
on the Mission
in East Timor*

Celia Mather

*Celia Mather is a writer
usually involved in
workers' education on the
global economy. She was a
United Nations Volunteer
who helped with the recent
popular consultation in
East Timor.*

As the world watched, a humiliated Indonesian Army and its militiamen went on a rampage of terror across East Timor. The East Timorese had resoundingly and courageously voted four out of five for independence, despite all the intimidation they had faced in the run-up to the vote on 30 August 1999. The Army and its henchmen were clearly determined to destroy whatever they could as they left.

The United Nations seemed completely wrong-footed. There to carry out the vote and then become the Transitional Authority to whatever new dispensation was voted for, it was then unable to prevent the murder of as yet uncounted thousands, and the utter destruction of dozens of towns and villages by burning and looting. Thousands fled into the mountains where they now face hunger and disease, especially with the rainy season starting.

Nor could the UN stop the forced removal of one-quarter of East Timor's population across the border into West Timor, where they are mostly in camps under the control of the militia and fearful for their lives and safety. The UN could not even safeguard its own staff – especially the East Timorese it recruited but also the one thousand UN officers, volunteers, foreign police and military personnel deployed for the vote – nor its premises, equipment and infrastructure worth millions of US dollars. It was in great danger of being seen to abandon defenceless people to their persecutors, and parallels were being drawn with Rwanda, Somalia and Bosnia.

I was one of the UN Volunteers sent to East Timor to help organise the vote. I did not stay the course as I got a lung infection and had to return home to England. So, like the rest of the world, I watched with wonder as the people went to the polls, and with utter dismay as the post-vote terror unfolded.

Many friends, family and journalists asked me in the weeks that followed, 'How could the UN get it so wrong?', a question that has plagued me too. As a mere 'footsoldier' in the exercise, I suspect that the answer is beyond my reach at international geo-political and diplomatic levels. But I have also searched and cross-examined my own experiences of the United Nations Mission in East Timor (UNAMET) for clues off the ground. How did the political decisions in New York and elsewhere translate into reality in the towns and villages of East Timor during this momentous period?

Deployed to a 'hot spot'

The UN knew early on that it would face extreme difficulties in places like Liquica and Maliana to the west, and Viqueque to the south, where the militia and Indonesian Army (TNI) had carried out terrible massacres during the preceding months. Even as we volunteers were being trained at the Royal Australian Airforce Base in Darwin, there were reports of militiamen stoning and brandishing machetes at the UNAMET staff already sent into towns on the border with West Timor.

In the first week of July, my team was deployed to villages mid-way along the southern coast. Our regional headquarters were in the mountain town of Same. We were told that this was a 'relatively safe' area, but this was not so. The local militia, called Ablai, had a stronghold in the mountain town of Alas. There had been a massacre in Alas a few months earlier and the church was providing sanctuary to hundreds. In Same too, hundreds had fled into the church compound. As we were to find out in the weeks that followed, militia bands were active in most of the villages in the mountains and on the coastal plains. Moving along the main roads in our UN jeep, we passed many Ablai posts, often not a stone's throw away from the local Indonesian army post. UNAMET in Dili later admitted that they had put my team in a very vulnerable situation, into a 'hot spot' that was not known to be one.

Our team was sent to cover three village units down on the plains, almost two hours' drive away from Same. As soon as we arrived in the central village, Besusu, our local staff – an interpreter, driver, clerk and queue controller – were nervous. 'This is not a good area', they said. I speak fluent Indonesian and soon realised they were right. At our first meeting, the village head was provocative and looked likely to bring us trouble. But our task was clear, to find a site for the registration/polling centre and get ready to open up on 16 July.

We settled on the local primary school and started visiting local hamlets and settlements to let the people know we had arrived. We shook hands with everyone. We got a lot of practical help. Farmers dug our jeep out of the mud and schoolteachers prepared our room. But everyone was guarded. We were all being watched. Nuns we met along the road whispered urgent warnings about the nightly intimidation of the villagers by Ablai. 'The people so badly need you here', said one before scurrying away. I looked at my team. There was me, a writer from the UK, with a basket-ball coach from India as my fellow District Electoral Officer (DEO), and a civilian police officer from Thailand as our 'CivPol', whose job it was to liaise with the Indonesian police. We hoped the people were not hoping for too much from us.

Our security was in the hands of 'Brimob', the Indonesian police's Mobile Brigade that is sent throughout Indonesia's troubled islands to crush rebellion and dissent. All day, and at night on our verandah, we were to be guarded by armed Brimob. We heard that the East Timorese felt sorry for us, the chickens being guarded by the fox.

All three village heads as well as the District Head (Camat) where we worked were in thick with the militia. Their plan seemed to be to get the people registered and then intimidate them into voting for autonomy within Indonesia. So, during registration there was a kind of nervous cooperation between us. They organised the villagers to join the queue, ostensibly so that few had to wait long in the heat. However, their command over the people was clear. They brought the lame, the sick and the apparently terrified who sat before us to answer our questions.

Our first job was to register the people and create an electoral roll of those entitled to vote. Name? Where were you born? Do you know when you were born? Do you have any documents? We wondered if we could ever convince these frightened young women bearing sick babies, and aged farmers who had barely ever held a pen before, of their right to vote freely and fairly, and that we could guarantee their safety to vote from their hearts. Were we off Mars?

Whichever way we turned, we felt the militia on our backs. The village heads penned us notes claiming that certain under-age youths were over seventeen, though the youths themselves did not know their own birthdates. They tried a number of aggressive challenges to the rules over proof of eligibility. But we could see they were also floundering to understand what we were doing and how to respond. We stuck doggedly to our tasks, urgently filling in forms as if this would keep back the chaos.

Sometimes the electoral rules played into the hands of the village heads. They were entitled to sign the 'Affidavits of Birth' that we handed out to the vast majority of our villagers to use as one of the two documents needed to prove eligibility. But we had to be flexible so as to register all those truly entitled to vote. Many had lost their church Book of Life and other papers. 'Burned by the military during the rebellion', they told us through our interpreter.

Half way through registration, the militia suddenly changed tactics. The first sign was a rumour that there was a price for the first one of the international staff in our area killed. The very next day, the militia in Besusu insisted that the Indonesian flag must be raised outside our room at the school. It was a deliberate provocation as we were not to have any insignia other than the UN logo within a certain radius. Despite agreement with the District Head that the flag could stay down, the village-level militia had their tails up, apparently on instruction 'from Same'. The schoolteachers were threatened overnight in fear of their lives and the next morning we found ourselves surrounded by thirty militiamen armed with long knives. There was no option but to close down and negotiate safe passage for our team. As so often happened to the UNAMET teams, our Brimob police guardians went missing at the time.

We decided to move to the neighbouring village of Dotik to register the people there. Only now we were in the hands of a slightly more clever band of militia than those in Besusu. In fact, the village head insisted on telling me he was an Ablai member but did not agree with 'the others in Besusu'. He told me that in case we had gone back to Besusu that day, an ambush had been set by the bridge. Rumour is a militia tactic, but it sounded like we had had a narrow escape.

In between such incidents, we DEOs registered non-stop. When they told us during our training in Darwin what was expected of us, our hearts sank. We had to register about one person every four minutes for eight hours a day (excluding lunch) for twenty days, later and cruelly (for us) extended by two. DEO fingers blistered and backs ached from the plastic bucket chairs. We wondered why we could not have a day off a week. We wondered why the UN had recruited exactly 400 DEOs for 200 centres, with no contingency for those, like me, who got sick. In fact, some fifty DEOs contracted malaria, one in eight, and more volunteers had to be drafted in.

Every fifth day we took our completed registration books to the regional centres. Our two hour drive to Same was along deeply rutted roads, past a number of militia posts. Men in Ablai T-shirts sat beside bamboo booms that could be lowered across the road. Such roadblocks were supposed to be abandoned, according to agreements signed with the UN.

From Same our books were helicoptered to the capital Dili and flown on to Sydney in Australia, to be put on computer. The UN does know how to run an election. A few elements were inappropriate. For example, the electoral list was put up in each area so that individuals could 'challenge' fraudulent entries, but this was hardly likely to happen in the context of such intimidation. However, overall I felt very confident in the electoral system. The many fail-safe mechanisms took the burden of confronting every last attempt at fraud away from the shoulders of us DEOs.

Where we lived was a village about twenty minutes' drive from where we worked. Also staying here was the team that registered this village, the DEOs coming from Uganda and Sierra Leone, the CivPol from Zimbabwe. This village, Fatuberliu, had a much healthier atmosphere. There was a strong church community. Children went to school in clean uniforms and boys played football on the field. There were reportedly some militia members but villagers said that they never dominated there as 'the people would not accept it'.

There was no open pro-independence activity in the villages where we worked but there was where we lived. One night we met some clandestine pro-independence activists through the church, and heard that they housed a Falantil guerrilla unit for a few nights as it passed through. I was later told that this was the only place for miles around where there was a public pro-independence rally during the campaign period. The District Head here was pro-autonomy but he was also a wily politician and seemingly a respected local leader. He and his family helped to house us and he organised villagers on a nightly rota to join, or perhaps to keep an eye on, the Brimob police playing cards on our verandah.

The UN had warned us of 'difficult living conditions' and gave us bottled drinking water and emergency food rations. We needed them. The economy was at a virtual standstill. Very few foodstuffs were being traded between the villages because people preferred to stay close to home. We were near the coast but there was almost no fish to buy. 'The fishermen are not going out to sea because of the security situation', we were told. The nightly terror patrols of the militia made many farmers too tired to tend their fields by day.

These villages on the coastal plain were largely made up of subsistence farmers. There were hardly any shops or roadside stalls, just an occasional small market. However, the land is fertile with a wide biodiversity according to the plant life we saw. The river beds are extremely large, carrying the massive rainfall from the mountains during the wet season. The sun shines and there seems plenty of land to feed the people, once there is security and economic life can begin again, and now that the vast amount of East Timor that is in the hands of ex-President Suharto and his cronies can be freed up.

Many of the older people of our villages were originally from the mountains. They had been pushed down by the Indonesian Army during the late 1970s and early 1980s in an attempt to remove the support bases for the guerrillas. Down on the coastal plains, hundreds died of starvation in the early 1980s before they could harvest their first crops. Gradually they settled and were given title to land. However, many still believe themselves to be the owners under customary law of land, coffee bushes and coconut trees in the mountains. Most of them have probably fled there now.

Also in our area were several agricultural transmigration camps (UPT). The Indonesian Government's Transmigration Programme transfers people around the different islands, supposedly as a way of providing land to the landless but also as a means of colonisation and pacification. The current Minister for Transmigration is Major General Hendropriyono, an army intelligence officer originally from the army special forces Kopassus which have been at the heart of terrorising East Timor.

The transmigration camps in our area housed people born locally, East Timorese from elsewhere in the territory, plus some Indonesians, especially from Atambua in West Timor. Religious teachers warned us about the intimidation in the camps. Some are quite remote, set back off the road by up to 10 kms, and were likely breeding grounds for the militia. The population in one was said to be down by about a third because many had fled to Dili in the month between the Indonesian general elections in June and our arrival.

UN responses to growing intimidation

As the registration period drew to a close and the campaigning period got under way, the militia stepped up their activities. What had been largely threats and posturing was turning into something much more ugly. Just as I was being helicoptered sick out of Same to the UNAMET clinic in Dili, Ablai militiamen surrounded the pro-independence activists trying to open a campaign office less than a mile away. Tension built up as the Brimob police failed to respond to UNAMET requests to disarm the militiamen, as per agreement. Eventually, an elderly man had his hand almost severed by a militia machete and ran bleeding profusely into a registration centre, seeking sanctuary.

As the education phase continued, more incidents tested the reactions of UNAMET. The District Electoral Officers' task now was to explain the nature of the ballot paper with its two choices, how the vote would actually be carried out, and how the UN would guarantee the secrecy of the vote. At the time, this seemed crucial if the people were to have the courage to ignore the intimidation and vote from their hearts. I now think they knew all along that the militia and the TNI would go on the rampage anyway, and despite this they were determined to tell the world what they really wanted – an end to Indonesian rule.

How did UNAMET in the regions respond to the increasingly nasty situation? What personnel and structures did it have in place to monitor, understand and confront the Indonesian Army, political apparatus, and militia on the ground? By what criteria had the UNAMET staff been recruited, how were their roles defined, and what training had they been given? Did they have the necessary competence and authority? Or, were my nagging worries coming true, that the Indonesian Army was setting traps and snares, testing and watching, and increasingly pleased by the weak responses?

There can be no doubt that in our region UNAMET's Military Liaison Officers (MLOs), Security Officer and many (though not all) of our Civilian Police Officers (CivPols) worked incredibly hard at a personal level to try to get a grip on the situation. A number of them faced great personal danger to secure the ballot boxes as well as lives. Some were in the rebellion in the UNAMET Compound in Dili when, disobeying orders, they refused to leave until several thousand East Timorese staff and citizens who had sought sanctuary were also flown to Darwin.

Yet in the mission they seem to have been given an impossible task. They had no powers of enforcement, no threats or sanctions. Their role was only to communicate with the Indonesian military and police, to keep reminding them of the various agreements between the Indonesian Government and the UN. Yet, unlike the Electoral Officers in the registration centres, many of the 40-plus Military Liaison Officers out in the regions had no interpreters. A few spoke Indonesian or Tetun. In our region, our head MLO was reliant on his Malaysian military colleague speaking Malay to the Indonesian army officers. Elsewhere, UN military officers were dependent on liaison with English-speaking Indonesian army officers.

This must have made it very difficult to interpret events and make any real impact on the Indonesian military. One could see the anger and frustration on the face of one British MLO interviewed on TV after he returned from Maliana, perhaps the worst militia-riddled town of all. He stated clearly to the world that the head of the Indonesian military with whom he had had to liaise was also the head of the militia in the region.

A Security Officer oversaw the security of the mission and its personnel in our region. There was also a CivPol whose job it was to liaise with the Indonesian police (POLRI) at regional level. They also had no interpreters. Liaison with the Indonesian Police was to be done through an English-speaking POLRI officer posted for the task. The POLRI chief in our region had been in Bosnia and 'therefore knew about UN missions', I was told as if this might make all go well. I thought it failed to understand the position of the Indonesian police, who are subordinate to the Army within the Indonesian armed forces. (The separation of the Indonesian police force from the armed forces has been announced as one of the democratic reforms, but has not yet made much progress.) Even the infamous Brimob anti-riot police force was unlikely to disarm the militia if this meant that the Army special forces Kopassus would be on their backs for it.

The third component of the UNAMET team at regional level was the electoral and administrative/logistics staff, headed by the Regional Electoral Officers (REOs). They were either UN permanent staff drawn from offices around the world or drafted in from a pool of contract personnel who work on UN missions. Their main role was electoral, to ensure that the vote was carried out smoothly. Yet in such a situation as East Timor this could never be just a technical exercise. They would need to understand and work in a highly political context.

I met only two REOs and so I hesitate to generalise, but in both cases I came to doubt their political capacity. One, upon hearing that I speak Indonesian and know the country well, asked me, 'Perhaps you could tell me, why do Indonesian government officials lie so much?' In the Indonesian context, this was a surprising question. I wondered what experience or training he had. He was placed as UNAMET's chief officer in one of the most dangerous regions on the border with West Timor. Today, the town that was his centre is virtually 100% reduced to rubble and empty of people.

I felt very insecure about the way my own REO responded to the political situation. At first he seemed, or at least said he was, reassured that the local government head (Bupati) was cooperative and 'on board'. He shrugged his shoulders when I told him that the Bupati was already campaigning in our area before the agreed period. Three weeks later he acknowledged that the Bupati was trying to subvert the vote through a disinformation campaign.

My greatest worries were naturally over security. After the flag incident at Besusu our team made a full written report which we were lucky to get hand delivered to the regional centre the same day. We included intelligence which I had gathered by talking to the village heads and militia leaders. This included the regional government structures with whom the militia were liaising. We made recommendations about the level of policing needed if our team was to keep the militia at bay and achieve a free and fair vote. When I left my team ten days later, my CivPol confirmed that he could see no steps that had been taken to achieve this. Instead, the Regional Head's response to the incident was to challenge me briskly about why we had moved village and I had to impress upon him the seriousness of the security situation. I heard later that it took ten days for my report to reach Dili, leaving the political and electoral officers there confused about the situation in our area.

Our region of Same was probably an exception. In other areas there were political officers whose role it was to monitor events carefully. We did not have one because for some reason Same was technically a sub-region of another region in the UNAMET structure. The one political officer based there could not possibly cover this size of territory. So, apart from the logistic nightmare that this administrative structure caused, it also gave our REO a political responsibility for which he had little time and probably little training.

As for the District Electoral Officers like myself, I had never met UN Volunteers before, not even known of their existence. There were few Western Europeans like myself among those recruited. Many were Africans, Asians and Eastern Europeans. They were astonishingly hard-working and tolerant of the most difficult conditions. Many had worked in such places as Rwanda, Angola, Cambodia and Bosnia before. No-one warned us beforehand, but perhaps one team in five was out of communication with family and friends at home for a month at a time. Some were helicoptered into remote mountain areas to stay for the duration.

Some teams had a wonderful time. Some working in villages under the control of the pro-independence Falantil told me how villagers sang and danced for them. By contrast, the teams in Liquica, home of the Red and White Iron militia, rebelled en masse, twice. UNAMET had insisted that all Liquica teams must stay in the same place for their security. The only suitable one was the church compound where the TNI/militia had massacred dozens in April. The bloody handprints of the dead were still on the walls.

Most DEOs had been involved in elections in dangerous situations before. Few, however, had any experience or knowledge of Indonesia and East Timor. I seemed to be one of the few who could speak Indonesian or knew the history of the occupation. Many times, other DEOs sought my advice to help explain situations. Strangely, there was a time when the UN Volunteers office in Bonn responsible for recruitment told me I had not been accepted because I 'did not have enough elections experience' and they 'were not prioritising Indonesian language/experience because few East Timorese speak Indonesian' which is simply not true.

During DEO training in Darwin, the emphasis was on procedures for carrying out the registration and vote, on technical matters. We were given a security briefing, but it was factually incorrect and woefully inadequate for the situation we were about to go into. I have looked back at my notes and found that I wrote, 'Civilian authorities: usually friendly. Military (TNI): wary but cordial. Police: secondary in pecking order and some subdued; some proactive; sometimes nervous of their task. Never refuse their protection.' The TNI 'wary but cordial'? How could we be told that?

As we were boarding the UN Hercules to Dili, we were handed an Australian Defence Force handbook on East Timor. It was only then that many DEOs were for the first time confronted with pictures of what they might face: militiamen brandishing homemade guns. You can't speak to each other in a deafening Hercules, but by their faces I could see the shock.

Political lessons

In organising a free and fair vote in East Timor within months, seizing a probably never-to-be-repeated offer from the outgoing Indonesian President Habibie, the UN moved at exceptional and impressive speed. The usual eighteen months' preparation for a vote was somehow compressed into just three. Some corners were bound to be cut. Many inadequacies in administration, logistics, recruitment, training, and so on could not be avoided.

Some believe that the UN was playing far too dangerous a game in even attempting the vote in such a short time. I take a different view. I believe the UN was right to seize the moment and to give the East Timorese what they were clamouring for – a chance to make their views known to the world – though the UN should never have accepted an Indonesian veto over the time-frame.

I do feel that the UN was playing fast and loose with our lives, but that this was more due to its political rather than administrative weaknesses. The 5 May Agreement with the Indonesian Government that gave the mission its mandate put the security of the popular consultation and the period after the vote in the hands of the Indonesian Government which could not or would not control its military forces on the ground. Perhaps this was the best that the UN and the Portuguese Government (which the UN formally still recognised as the administering authority) could negotiate from the Indonesian Government. Others will be able to judge how hard the UN did in fact try, or was allowed to try by its member governments.

The UN cannot have been limited by the quality of information at its disposal about the security situation. Numerous East Timorese, from Bishop Belo to the CNRT liberation movement, had tried to tell the world that there would likely be a bloodbath. The UN's own political officers in the regions were making reports to Dili, and Dili to New York. The intelligence capacities of its member governments should have told the UN that the Indonesian Government was preparing ships, trucks and camps for the forcible removal of the population, and so on. The question rather is what the UN chose or was allowed by its member governments to do with this information. So many times, the choice seemed to be capitulation to Indonesian sensibilities rather than taking a firm stand against a brutal occupying force that was planning terror.

In this article I have been trying to describe and analyse how these political weaknesses translated onto the ground. The terms of the 5 May Agreement meant that we had unarmed military and police officers in place who did not have the political or technical tools to secure anyone's safety. For reasons that are still unclear to me, we had electoral officers who focused on the vote as a technical process but had insufficient experience or training to understand the political context in which they were working. We UN Volunteers were given very inadequate training on the security situation we had to face. We were even misled. That no international UN staff were killed must have been a decision taken by the Indonesian authorities.

What the Indonesian Army and its militia had in mind for the East Timorese was, by contrast, utter terror. It was an open secret that the UN's local staff would be targetted after the vote. Our team's interpreter was openly threatened in my presence. He is now safe in Darwin, along with his brother, helped to leave by some very brave military and police officers rather than by UN planning. They have no news whatsoever of their families in Same. Our driver disappeared in Dili, and our clerk or queue controller were last seen in Same. I hear that in Same the Indonesian army and militia had trucks at the ready to force people down to the southern coast and onto ships to be taken away to West Timor. It may be a long time before the UN and I know what happened to my team's staff.

I know from email messages now flying around the world that others who were with UNAMET in East Timor share my hope that somehow the UN and its member governments will be able to learn some political lessons in time for the UN's next missions elsewhere in the world.

Glossary

United Nations
UNAMET	United Nations Mission in East Timor
MLO	Military Liaison Officer
CivPol	Civilian Police liaison officer
REO	Regional Electoral Officer
DEO	District Electoral Officer
UNV	United Nations Volunteer

Indonesia
TNI	Tentara Nasional Indonesia, Indonesian Armed Forces
Kopassus	Army Special Forces
POLRI	Indonesian Police Force
Brimob	Brigade Mobile, Police Mobile Brigade
Bupati	Regional local government head
Camat	District local government head
Ablai	Militia in the Same region
UPT	Transmigration Camp

East Timor
CNRT	National Council for Timorese Resistance

Ethical Imperialism
The war after the war
(*Spokesman* 65)

Contributors include Harold Pinter, Ken Coates (editor), Noam Chomsky, Zhores A. Medvedev, Pedro Marset Campos MEP & Michael Barratt Brown.

After the Yugoslav War, Europe will not be the same again. It was claimed that the war was launched to defend human rights. But the pretensions of 'ethical imperialism' are nakedly exposed by disregard for human rights elsewhere in the world.

ISBN 0 85124 625 7
Price £5.00

'I've just had a chance to read the issue of *The Spokesman* on *Ethical Imperialism*. It's really first-rate.'

Noam Chomsky

*   *   *

Our next issue, *Spokesman* 67, will focus on the problems created by depleted uranium, analysing its use in Iraq and the war against Yugoslavia. Felicity Arbuthnot, whose investigative journalism has done much to shed light on the terrible effects on health of these weapons, brings an eyewitness report from Iraq.

*   *   *

Copies of *The Spokesman*, including back issues, are available from **Russell House, Bulwell Lane, Nottingham NG6 0BT, England**.

Please send payment with order (£5 plus 50p carriage per issue in UK, £5 plus £1 carriage per issue ex-UK).

Cheques payable to 'Bertrand Russell House'

The Third Way

Europe: The Third Way/ Die Neue Mitte

Tony Blair and Gerhard Schroeder

On the 8th June 1999, in London, British Prime Blair and German Chancellor Schroeder made a joint declaration of policy for Europe.

Introduction

Social democrats are in government in almost all the countries of the European Union. Social democracy has found new acceptance – but only because, while retaining its traditional values, it has begun in a credible way to renew its ideas and modernise its programmes. It has also found new acceptance because it stands not only for social justice but also for economic dynamism and the unleashing of creativity and innovation.

The trademark of this approach is the New Centre in Germany and the Third Way in the United Kingdom. Other social democrats choose other terms that suit their own national cultures. But though the language and the institutions may differ, the motivation is everywhere the same. Most people have long since abandoned the world view represented by the dogmas of left and right. Social democrats must be able to speak to those people.

Fairness and social justice, liberty and equality of opportunity, solidarity and responsibility to others – these values are timeless. Social democracy will never sacrifice them. To make these values relevant to today's world requires realistic and forward-looking policies capable of meeting the challenges of the 21st century. Modernisation is about adapting to conditions that have objectively changed, and not reacting to polls.

Similarly, we need to apply our politics within a new economic framework, modernised for today, where government does all it can to support enterprise but never believes it is a substitute for enterprise. The essential function of markets must be complemented and improved by political action, not hampered by it. We support a market economy, not a market society.

We share a common destiny within the European Union. We face the same challenges – to promote employment and prosperity, to offer every individual the opportunity to fulfil their unique potential, to combat social exclusion and poverty, to reconcile material progress with environmental sustainability and our responsibility to future generations, to tackle common problems that threaten the cohesion of society such as crime and drugs, and to make Europe a more effective force for good in the world.

We need to strengthen our policies by benchmarking our experiences in Britain and Germany, but also with like-minded counterparts in Europe and the rest of the world. We must learn from each other and measure our own performance against best practice and experience in other countries. With this appeal, we invite other European social democratic governments who share our modernising aims to join us in this enterprise.

I. Learning from experience

Although both parties can be proud of our historic achievements, today we must develop realistic and feasible answers to new challenges confronting our societies and economies. This requires adherence to our values but also a willingness to change our old approaches and traditional policy instruments in the past:

– The promotion of social justice was sometimes confused with the imposition of equality of outcome. The result was a neglect of the importance of rewarding effort and responsibility, and the association of social democracy with conformity and mediocrity rather that the celebration of creativity, diversity and excellence. Work was burdened with ever higher costs.

– The means of achieving social justice became identified with ever higher levels of public spending regardless of what they achieved or the impact of the taxes required to fund it on competitiveness, employment and living standards. Decent public services are a vital concern for social democrats, but social conscience cannot be measured by the level of public expenditure. The real test for society is how effectively this expenditure is used and how much it enables people to help themselves.

– The belief that the state should address damaging market failures all too often led to a disproportionate expansion of the government's reach and the bureaucracy that went with it. The balance between the individual and the collective was distorted. Values that are important to citizens, such as personal achievement and success, entrepreneurial spirit, individual responsibility and community spirit, were too often subordinated to universal social safeguards.

– Too often rights were elevated above responsibilities, but the responsibility of the individual to his or her family, neighbourhood and society cannot be offloaded on to the state. If the concept of mutual obligation is forgotten, this results in a decline in community spirit, lack of responsibility towards neighbours, rising crime and vandalism, and a legal system that cannot cope.

– The ability of national governments to fine-tune the economy in order to secure growth and jobs has been exaggerated. The importance of individual and business enterprise to the creation of wealth has been undervalued. The weaknesses of markets have been overstated and their strengths underestimated.

II. New programmes for changed realities

Ideas of what is 'left-wing' should never become an ideological straitjacket.

The politics of the New Centre and Third Way is about addressing the concerns of people who live and cope with societies undergoing rapid change – both winners and losers. In this newly emerging world people want politicians who approach issues without ideological preconceptions and who, applying their values and principles, search for practical solutions to their problems through honest well-constructed and pragmatic policies. Voters who in their daily lives have to display initiative and adaptability in the face of economic and social change expect the same from their governments and their politicians.

– In a world of ever more rapid globalisation and scientific changes we need to create the conditions in which existing businesses can prosper and adapt, and new businesses can be set up and grow.

– New technologies radically change the nature of work and internationalise the organisation of production. With one hand they de-skill and make some businesses obsolete, with another they create new business and vocational opportunities. The most important task of modernisation is to invest in human capital: to make the individual and businesses fit for the knowledge-based economy of the future.

– Having the same job for life is a thing of the past. Social democrats must accommodate the growing demands for flexibility – and at the same time maintain minimum social standards, help families to cope with change and open up fresh opportunities for those who are unable to keep pace.

– We face an increasing challenge in reconciling environmental responsibility towards future generations with material progress for society at large. We must marry environmental responsibility with a modern market-based approach. In environmental protection, the most modern technologies consume fewer resources, open up new markets and create new jobs.

– Public expenditure as a proportion of national income has more or less reached the limits of acceptability. Constraints on 'tax and spend' force radical modernisation of the public sector and reform of public services to achieve better value for money. The public sector must actually serve the citizen: we do not hesitate to promote the concepts of efficiency, competition and high performance.

– Social security systems need to adapt to changes in life expectancy, family structures and the role of women. Social democrats need to find ways of combating the ever more pressing problems of crime, social disintegration and drug abuse. We need to take the lead in shaping a society with equal rights for women and men.

– Crime is a vital political issue for modern social democrats. We consider safety on the street to be a civil right. A policy to make cities worth living in fosters community spirit, creates new jobs and makes residential areas safer.

– Poverty remains a central concern, especially among families with children. We need specific measures for those who are most threatened by marginalisation and social exclusion.

This also requires a modern approach to government:

– The state should not row, but steer; not so much control, as challenge. Solutions to problems must be joined up.

– Within the public sector bureaucracy at all levels must be reduced, performance targets and objectives formulated, the quality of public services rigorously monitored, and bad performance rooted out.

– Modern social democrats solve problems where they can best be solved. Some problems can now only be tackled at European level: others, such as the recent financial crises, require increased international co-operation. But, as a general principle, power should be devolved to the lowest possible level.

For the new politics to succeed, it must promote a go-ahead mentality and a new entrepreneurial spirit at all levels of society. That requires:

– a competent and well-trained workforce eager and ready to take on new responsibilities

– a social security system that opens up new opportunities and encourages initiative, creativity and readiness to take on new challenges

– a positive climate for entrepreneurial independence and initiative. Small businesses must become easier to set up and better able to survive

– we want a society which celebrates successful entrepreneurs just as it does artists and footballers – and which values creativity in all spheres of life.

Our countries have different traditions in dealings between state, industry, trade unions and social groups, but we share a conviction that traditional conflicts at the workplace must be overcome. This, above all, means rekindling a spirit of community and solidarity, strengthening partnership and dialogue between all groups in society and developing a new consensus for change and reform. We want all groups in society to share our joint commitment to the new directions set out in this Declaration.

Immediately upon taking office, the new Social Democratic government in Germany gathered the top representatives of the political sector, the business community and the unions around the table to forge an Alliance for Jobs, Training and Competitiveness.

– We want to see real partnership at work, with employees having the opportunity of sharing the rewards of success with employers.

– We support modern trade unions protecting individuals against arbitrary behaviour, and working in co-operation with employers to manage change and create long-term prosperity.

– In Europe – under the umbrella of a European employment pact – we will strive to pursue an ongoing dialogue with the social partners that supports, not hinders, necessary economic change.

III. A new supply-side agenda for the left

The task facing Europe is to meet the challenge of the global economy while maintaining social cohesion in the face of real and perceived uncertainty. Rising employment and expanding job opportunities are the best guarantee of a cohesive society.

The past two decades of neo-liberal laissez-faire are over. In its place, however, there must not be a renaissance of 1970s-style reliance on deficit spending and heavy-handed state intervention. Such an approach now points in the wrong direction.

Our national economies and global economic relationships have undergone profound change. New conditions and new realities call for a re-evaluation of old ideas and the development of new concepts.

In much of Europe unemployment is far too high – and a high proportion of it is structural. To address this challenge, Europe's social democrats must together formulate and implement a new supply-side agenda for the left.

Our aim is to modernise the welfare state, not dismantle it: to embark on new ways of expressing solidarity and responsibility to others without basing the motivation for economic activity on pure undiluted self-interest.

The main elements of this approach are as follows.

A robust and competitive market framework

Product market competition and open trade is essential to stimulate productivity and growth. For that reason a framework that allows market forces to work properly is essential to economic success and a pre-condition of a more successful employment policy.

– The EU should continue to act as a resolute force for liberalisation of world trade.

– The EU should build on the achievements of the single market to strengthen an economic framework conducive to productivity growth.

A tax policy to promote sustainable growth

In the past social democrats became identified with high taxes, especially on business. Modern social democrats recognise that in the right circumstances, tax reform and tax cuts can play a critical part in meeting their wider social objectives.

For instance, corporate tax cuts raise profitability and strengthen the incentives to invest. Higher investment expands economic activity and increases productive potential. It helps create a virtuous circle of growth increasing the resources available for public spending on social purposes.

– The taxation of companies should be simplified and corporation tax rates cut, as they have been by New Labour in the UK and are planned by the federal government in Germany.

– To ensure work pays and to improve the fairness of the tax system, the tax burden borne by working families and workers should be alleviated, as begun in

Germany (through the Tax Relief Act) – and the introduction of lower starting rates of income tax and the working families tax credit in Britain.

– The willingness and ability of enterprises – especially small and medium-sized enterprises – to invest should be enhanced, as intended by the Social Democratic government in Germany through the reform of the taxes on businesses and as shown by New Labour's reform of capital gains and business taxes in Britain.

– Overall, the taxation of hard work and enterprise should be reduced. The burden of taxation should be rebalanced, for example towards environmental 'bads'. Germany, the UK and other European countries governed by social democrats will lead the way in this regard.

– At EU level, tax policy should support tough action to combat unfair competition and fight tax evasion. This requires enhanced co-operation, not uniformity. We will not support measures leading to a higher tax burden and jeopardising competitiveness and jobs in the EU.

Demand and supply-side policies go together – they are not alternatives
In the past social democrats often gave the impression that the objectives of growth and high unemployment would be achieved by successful demand management alone. Modern social democrats recognise that supply side policies have a central and complementary role to play.

In today's world most policy decisions have an impact on both supply- and demand-side conditions.

– Successful Welfare to Work programmes raise incomes for those previously out of work as well as improve the supply of labour available to employers.

– Modern economic policy aims to increase the after-tax income of workers and at the same time decrease the costs of labour to the employer. The reduction of non-wage labour costs through structural reform of social security systems and a more employment friendly tax and contribution structure that looks to the future is therefore of particular importance.

The aim of social democratic policy is to overcome the apparent contradiction between demand- and supply-side policies in favour of a fruitful combination of micro-economic flexibility and macro-economic stability.

To achieve higher growth and more jobs in today's world, economies must be adaptable: flexible markets are a modern social democratic aim.

Macro-economic policy still has a vital purpose: to set the conditions for stable growth and avoid boom and bust. But social democrats must recognise that getting the macro-economics right is not sufficient to stimulate higher growth and more jobs. Changes in interest rates or tax policy will not lead to increased investment and employment unless the supply side of the economy is adaptable enough to respond. To make the European economy more dynamic, we also need to make it more flexible.

– Companies must have room for manoeuvre to take advantage of improved economic conditions and seize new opportunities they must not be gagged by rules and regulations.

– Product, capital and labour markets must all be flexible: we must not combine rigidity in one part of the economic system with openness and dynamism in the rest.

Adaptability and flexibility are at an increasing premium in the knowledge-based service economy of the future

Our economies are in transition – from industrial production to the knowledge-based service economy of the future. Social democrats must seize the opportunity of this radical economic change. It offers Europe a chance to catch up with the United States. It offers millions of our people the chance to find new jobs, learn new skills, pursue new careers, set up and expand new businesses – in summary, to realise their hopes of a better future.

But social democrats have to recognise that the basic requirements for economic success have changed. Services cannot be kept in stock: customers use them as and when they are needed – at many different times of day, outside what people think of as normal working hours. The rapid advance of the information age, especially the huge potential of electronic commerce, promises to change radically the way we shop, the way we learn, the way we communicate and the way we relax. Rigidity and over-regulation hamper our success in the knowledge-based service economy of the future. They will hold back the potential of innovation to generate new growth and more jobs. We need to become more flexible, not less.

An active government, in a newly conceived role, has a key role to play in economic development

Modern social democrats are not laissez-faire neo-liberals. Flexible markets must be combined with a newly defined role for an active state. The top priority must be investment in human and social capital.

If high employment is to be achieved and sustained, employees must react to shifting demands. Our economies suffer from a considerable discrepancy between the number of job vacancies that need to be filled (for example in the field of information and communication technology) and the number of suitably qualified applicants.

That means education must not be a 'one-off' opportunity: lifetime access to education and training and lifelong utilisation of their opportunities represent the most important security available in the modern world. Therefore, governments have a responsibility to put in place a framework that enables individuals to enhance their qualifications and to fulfil their potential. This must now be a top social democratic priority.

– Standards at all levels of schooling and for all abilities of pupils must be raised. Where there are problems of literacy and numeracy these must be addressed, otherwise we condemn unskilled individuals to lives of low pay, insecurity and unemployment.

– We want all young people to have the opportunity to gain entry into the world of work by means of qualified vocational training. Together with local employers, trade unions and others, we must ensure that sufficient education and training opportunities are available to meet the requirements of the local labour market. In Germany, the political sector is supporting this endeavour with an immediate action programme for jobs and training that will enable 100,000 young people to find a new job or training place or to obtain qualifications. In Britain the Welfare to Work programme has already enabled 95,000 young people to find work.

– We need to reform post-school education and raise its quality, at the same time modernising education and training programmes so as to promote adaptability and employability in later life. Government has a particular role in providing incentives for individuals to save in order to meet the costs of lifelong learning – and in widening access through the promotion of distance learning.

– We should ensure that training plays a significant role in our active labour market policies for the unemployed and workless households.

A modern and efficient public infrastructure including a strong scientific base is also an essential feature of a job-generating economy. It is important to ensure that the composition of public expenditure is being directed at activities most beneficial to growth and fostering necessary structural change.

Modern social democrats should be champions of small and medium-sized enterprise

The development of prosperous small and medium-sized businesses has to be a top priority for modern social democrats. Here lies the biggest potential for new growth and jobs in the knowledge-based society of the future.

People in many different walks of life are looking for the opportunity to become entrepreneurs – long-standing as well as newly self-employed people, lawyers, computer experts, medical doctors, craftsmen, business consultants, people active in culture and sport. These individuals must have scope to develop economic initiative and create new business ideas. They must be encouraged to take risks. The burdens on them must be lightened. Their markets and their ambitions must not be hindered by borders.

– Europe's capital markets should be opened up so that growing firms and entrepreneurs can have ready access to finance. We intend to work together to ensure that growing high-tech firms enjoy the same access to the capital markets as their US rivals.

– We should make it easy for individuals to set up businesses and for new companies to grow by lightening administrative burdens, exempting small businesses from onerous regulations and widening access to finance. We should make it easier for small businesses in particular to take on new staff: that means lowering the burden of regulation and non-wage labour costs.

– The links between business and the science base should be strengthened to ensure more entrepreneurial 'spin offs' from research and the promotion of 'clusters' of new high-tech industries.

Sound public finance should be a badge of pride for social democrats

In the past, social democrats have all too often been associated with the view that the best way to promote employment and growth is to increase government borrowing in order to finance higher government spending. We do not rule out government deficits – during a cyclical downturn it makes sense to let the automatic stabilisers work. And borrowing to finance higher government investment, in strict accordance with the Golden Rule, can play a key role in strengthening the supply side of the economy.

However, deficit spending cannot be used to overcome structural weaknesses in the economy that are a barrier to faster growth and higher employment. Social democrats also must not tolerate excessive levels of public sector debt. Increased indebtedness represents an unfair burden on future generations. It could have unwelcome redistributive effects. Above all, money spent on servicing high public sector debt is not available to be spent on other priorities, including increased investment in education, training or the transport infrastructure.

From the standpoint of a supply-side policy of the left, it is essential that high levels of government borrowing decrease and not increase.

IV. An active labour market policy for the left

The state must become an active agent for employment, not merely the passive recipient of the casualties of economic failure.

People who have never had experience of work or who have been out of work for long periods lose the skills necessary to compete in the labour market. Prolonged unemployment also damages individual life chances in other ways and makes it more difficult for individuals to participate fully in society.

A welfare system that puts limits on an individual's ability to find a job must be reformed.

Modern social democrats want to transform the safety net of entitlements into a springboard to personal responsibility.

For our societies, the imperatives of social justice are more than the distribution of cash transfers. Our objective is the widening of equality of opportunity, regardless of race, age or disability, to fight social exclusion and ensure equality between men and women.

People rightly demand high-quality public services and solidarity for all who need help – but also fairness towards those who pay for it. All social policy instruments must improve life chances, encourage self-help and promote personal responsibility.

With this aim in mind, the health care system and the system for ensuring financial security in old age are being thoroughly modernised in Germany by adapting both to the changes in life expectancy and changing lifelong patterns of employment, without sacrificing the principle of solidarity. The same thinking applies to the introduction of stakeholder pensions and the reform of disability benefits in Britain.

Periods of unemployment in an economy without jobs for life must become an opportunity to attain qualifications and foster personal development. Part-time work and low-paid work are better than no work because they ease the transition from unemployment to jobs.

New policies to offer unemployed people jobs and training are a social democratic priority – but we also expect everyone to take up the opportunity offered.

But providing people with the skills and abilities to enter the workforce is not enough. The tax and benefits systems need to make sure it is in people's interests to work. A streamlined and modernised tax and benefits system is a significant component of the left's active supply-side labour market policy. We must:

– Make work pay for individuals and families. The biggest part of the income must remain in the pockets of those who worked for it.

– Encourage employers to offer 'entry' jobs to the labour market by lowering the burden of tax and social security contributions on low-paid jobs. We must explore the scope to lower the burden of non-wage labour costs by environmental taxes.

– Introduce targeted programmes for the long-term unemployed and other disadvantaged groups to give them the opportunity to reintegrate into the labour market on the principle of rights and responsibilities going together.

– Assess all benefit recipients, including people of working age in the receipt of disability benefits, for their potential to earn, and reform state employment services to assist those capable of work to find appropriate work.

– Support enterprise and setting up an own business as a viable route out of unemployment. Such decisions contain considerable risks for those who dare to make such a step. We must support those people by managing these risks.

The left's supply-side agenda will hasten structural change. But it will also make that change easier to live with and manage.

Adapting to change is never easy and the speed of change appears faster than ever before, not least under the impact of new technologies. Change inevitably destroys some jobs, but it creates others.

However, there can be lags between job losses in one sector and the creation of new jobs elsewhere. Whatever the longer-term benefits for economies and living standards, particular industries and communities can experience the costs before the gains. Hence we must focus our efforts on easing localised problems of transition. The dislocating effects of change will be greater the longer they are resisted, but it is no good pretending that they can be wished away.

Adjustment will be the easier, the more labour and product markets are working properly. Barriers to employment in relatively low productivity sectors need to be lowered if employees displaced by the productivity gains that are an inherent feature of structural change are to find jobs elsewhere. The labour market needs a low-wage sector in order to make low-skill jobs available. The tax and benefits system can replenish low incomes from employment and at the same time save on support payments for the unemployed.

V. Political benchmarking in Europe

The challenge is the definition and implementation of a new social democratic politics in Europe. We do not advocate a single European model, still less the transformation of the European Union into a superstate. We are pro-Europe and pro-reform in Europe. People will support further steps towards integration where there is real value-added and they can be clearly justified – such as action to combat crime and destruction of the environment as well as the promotion of common goals in social and employment policy. But at the same time Europe urgently needs reform – more efficient and transparent institutions, reform of outdated policies and decisive action against waste and fraud.

We are presenting our ideas as an outline, not a finalised programme. The politics of the New Centre and the Third Way is already a reality in many city councils, in reformed national policies, in European co-operation and in new international initiatives.

To this end the German and British governments have decided to embed their existing arrangements for exchanging views on policy development in a broader approach. We propose to do this in three ways:

– First, there will be a series of ministerial meetings, supported by frequent contacts among their close staff.

– We will seek discussion with political leaders in other European countries who wish to take forward with us modernising ideas for social democracy in their respective national contexts. We will start on this now.

– We will establish a network of experts, farsighted thinkers, political fora and discussion meetings. We will thereby deepen and continually further develop the concept of the New Centre and the Third Way. This is the priority for us.

The aim of this declaration is to give impetus to modernisation. We invite all social democrats in Europe not to let this historic opportunity for renewal pass by. The diversity of our ideas is our greatest asset for the future. Our societies expect us to knit together our diverse experiences in a new coherent programme.

Let us together build social democracy's success for the new century. Let the politics of the Third Way and the Neue Mitte be Europe's new hope.

The Third Way to the Servile State

Ken Coates &
Michael Barratt Brown

Ken Coates & Michael Barratt Brown are the authors of The Blair Revelation: Deliverance for whom? *(Spokesman Books, £6.99), and other criticisms of the neo-liberal policies which are now being advanced by the New Labour Government.*

The Third Way is now officially celebrated in the joint compact between Tony Blair and Gerhard Schroeder.

Their declaration begins with the triumphant affirmation that *'social democrats are in Government in almost all the countries'* of the European Union. This fact they attribute to their own virtue, in 'retaining traditional values', while beginning in a credible way 'to renew ideas ... and modernise ... programmes'. This modernisation is supposed to reflect the fact that *'most people have long since abandoned the world view represented by the dogmas of left and right'*.

What, then, are 'values' and what are 'dogmas'? Are dogmas simply values that have been junked? In which case, are values simply dogmas that we do not yet know how to junk? No, we are told: fairness and social justice, liberty and equality of opportunity, solidarity and responsibility to others: these are timeless values. Social democracy will never sacrifice them. Such claims invite sceptical analysis, at least. They may well also provoke anger.

It is extremely doubtful whether high expectations of fairness were active considerations among any but the merest fraction of the voters who recently displaced Chancellor Kohl and John Major in order to bring Mr Schroeder and Mr Blair to office. The defeat of Chancellor Kohl surely had little to do with any perception that he was more unfair than his successor. Indeed, in what particular has Mr Blair shown himself to be fairer than John Major? Mass unemployment surely fosters a sense of grievance, and the late John Smith, as well as Oskar Lafontaine, inspired confidence that they would seek remedies for unemployment, alongside changes which might really offer a better future to the several million victims of the malfunctioning of capitalist society.

But the Third Way recognises no such malfunction. If capitalism fails to deliver, the problem is our own: we must adjust to it, *'adapt to conditions that have objectively changed'*. Government *'does all it can to support enterprise but never believes it is a substitute for enterprise'*. What does this mean? It seems that if our people are being throttled by Adam Smith's invisible hands, the Modern Third Way will get it over with more efficiently.

A new and an old Middle Way

A 'Third' or 'Middle Way' is not a new idea in politics. Once, however, it did not pretend to set enterprise free, but rather to steer it for the better. When Harold MacMillan in 1938 published his book entitled 'The Middle Way', it was based very largely on John Maynard Keynes's exploration of the philosophy as well as the economics of a middle way between unregulated capitalism and state socialism. Much of the language of the Blair-Schroeder manifesto is reminiscent of Keynes's political writing, which his biographer Lord Skidelsky claims to have shown him always 'engaged in a dialogue with the Labour movement'. But there the similarity ends. Keynes and MacMillan were fundamentally concerned with extending the regulation of capitalism. Blair and Schroeder are concerned with reducing it.

The manifesto claims in almost every paragraph to be a programme for a 'modern' social democracy to meet the requirements for a (largely undefined) 'modernisation' of both economy and society. What is said to be new and requiring adaptation to changed conditions is summarised under five main headings:

- 'ever more rapid globalisation and scientific changes'
- 'having the same job for life is a thing of the past'
- 'environmental responsibility'
- 'public expenditure as a proportion of national income has more or less reached the limits of acceptability'
- 'changes in life expectancy, family structures and the role of women'

Two of these assumptions are false, and the conclusions drawn from the other three can be questioned. There is no doubt about globalisation, but the response can be shown to be wholly mistaken. As for jobs for life, we shall show that careful studies by the International Labour Office conclude that 'the recent past was not a period of increased job instability.' What was happening was not that full-time jobs were lasting less long but that full time jobs were being lost and replaced by part-time jobs, especially for women. Environmental responsibility is certainly a very serious requirement of governments, but having mentioned it the manifesto says no more than that the 'burden of taxation should be rebalanced, for example towards environmental 'bads'. Government taxes and social security contributions in Europe have on average certainly risen as a proportion of national income since the 1980s, but this is mainly due to sharp rises in Italy and Spain, where they were very low. In Britain and Germany the proportion has fallen. And what is acceptable evidently varies greatly from country to country, as may be seen in Table 1. Changes in life expectancy, family structures and the role of women have undoubtedly been taking place, but these cannot be used as an argument for reducing welfare expenditure, only for redirecting it.

Globalisation of production and investment is certainly the main new factor affecting government policies, but the only comment on this in the Blair-Schroeder manifesto is that 'we need to create the conditions in which existing businesses can prosper and new businesses can be set up and grow'. The new element in globalisation is the enormous increase in short-term capital movements, many of which are purely speculative. But there is in fact no mention in the manifesto of these movements which even in the 1930s so much troubled Keynes, and this is despite the fact that Eastern Asia, Russia and Brazil have barely emerged from a deep crisis resulting from just such uncontrolled movements, whose influence on the global economy is not yet at an end.

Is there nothing to be said about this crisis and the vast increase in speculative activity that is indeed a new circumstance that requires adaptation? The whole thrust of the Anglo-German argument favours deregulation, not only about opening up the European market, but about the European Union continuing to act 'as a resolute force for liberalisation of world trade'. There is in the manifesto no recognition of the poorer countries' foreign debt problems, which Keynes only too clearly foresaw. He believed that there was an inevitable deflationary tendency in the international monetary system, and consequent political instability, because of the inequality between the small debtor countries and the large creditors in making adjustments in their accounts.

In drawing up the rules for the IMF, Keynes specifically allowed for capital controls even in an open international economy that facilitated foreign investment. In 1997, however, the IMF's constitution was amended to make 'the promotion of capital account liberalisation a specific purpose of the IMF' and 'to make unrestricted capital flows a condition of membership of the global economy' – a requirement that Mr Blair has repeatedly recommended – again despite the disastrous results of such unrestricted flows in East Asia and Russia.

How to conceal your true meaning

There is evidently a vast difference between the old Middle Way and the *Neue Mitte*. The latest version only uses the words of the old to provide cover for what is no more than an argument for continuing the process of deregulation: 'decreasing the costs of labour to the employer.' And the link to the so-called 'reform' of the welfare system is made clear. 'The reduction of non-wage labour costs through structural reform of social security systems and a more employment friendly tax and contribution structure...' are to be the aims of 'modern economic policy'. 'A fruitful combination of micro-economic flexibility and macro-economic stability' is to be the 'aim of social democratic policy'. This can be translated as weak labour protection by trade unions combined with strong government defence of capital through sound public finance – an active labour market policy on the supply side, but no state guarantees of full employment on the demand side.

This is a total reversion to a pre-Keynesian capitalism. For Keynes four essential elements characterised the Middle Way – ending unregulated capitalism and especially unregulated short term capital movements; ensuring a not too unequal distribution of income; within these two, freedom should be allowed for the market mechanism; and finally the Middle Way implies a philosophy that regards material wealth as a means and not an end. Keynes believed in income distribution as a major determinant of economic activity. He called himself a 'leveller' and declared that he wanted 'to mould a society in which most of the existing inequalities and causes of inequality are removed.' This was both for political and economic reasons. In a recent review of Keynes's writings, Jonathan Kirshner has found in a 1937 essay by Keynes for *The Eugenics Review* the robust claim that 'the maintenance of prosperity and civil peace are absolutely dependent on more equal distribution of income.'

Thus, the abandonment by New Labour of policies designed to reduce inequalities through measures of income redistribution is not only morally reprehensible but politically and economically damaging. This is all the more so at a time when inequalities have for some time been growing not only in Britain but world-wide. The evidence is well established. In the UK, while average earnings have been rising by about 5% a year, directors' pay rises have exceeded 10%, with many fat cats getting much higher figures. Even after taxes and benefits, the top fifth of households shared 44% of total final incomes in 1997-8 compared with 37% in 1979 and the bottom fifth shared 7%, in place of 9%. The share of privately owned wealth held by the top 10% of owners fell during the 1970s and 80s, but has recovered in the 1990s to its earlier level of 50%. The share of the bottom 50% of owners remains at 8%.

The causes of inequality

The immediate causes of the increase of inequalities are several. In a long period of economic growth in the industrialised countries profits have been rising faster than wages. In many countries, despite the economic growth, unemployment has been increasing. Even where it has not, men have been falling out of the labour force. One third of all men in the UK who are over 50 but below pension age have no paid work and most have given up seeking it. Much of the increased disparities can be attributed to the adoption by governments after the 1970s of monetarist policies designed to preserve the value of money, in place of Keynesian policies designed to maintain full employment. Capital accumulation at the expense of full employment inevitably means a widening gap between the wealth of owners of capital and the incomes of the labour force, whether employed or not.

But this tendency has been greatly aggravated by the globalisation of capital movements both for production and speculation. Concentration of finance for production and distribution in the hands of a small number of giant corporations operating transnationally has reduced the bargaining power not only of labour but of small nation states and small businesses, including in particular the millions of small-scale commodity producers in the ex-colonial countries. The economies of these countries in what we call the Third World, which had begun to catch up with the industrialised ex-colonial powers, went into decline after the 1970s, with the exception of a few East Asian tigers, which had Japanese influence and support. Elsewhere, not only did inequality grow between countries, but inequalities grew equally inside both the rich industrialised countries and the poor non-industrialised.

As capital was accumulated in the giant transnational companies at the expense of reduced purchasing power of workers and small-scale producers, company mergers and take-overs have proliferated to reduce labour costs and capture a shrinking market. In what is called 'the third industrial revolution' capitalism is being reshaped across nation state boundaries. In the first six months of 1999 completed mergers and acquisitions have reached $409 billion in value. As Alex Brummer in *The Guardian* (20.07.99) commented,

> 'It is as if half the total wealth of Britain changed hands in half a year. Britain was a big participant. British companies bought assets worth $139 billion – making them responsible for 48% of cross border deals, according to KPMG Corporate Finance.'

Giant companies can increase their profits without increasing their sales or their labour force. At the same time, the technological revolution has made possible still further reductions of labour requirements and of labour skills. A surplus of capital has emerged seeking investment world-wide, using the cheapest labour with the least non-labour costs, which include social provision and the costs of training and of safety, health and environmental regulations. The industries of the old industrial countries have found themselves challenged by production in China and East Asia. Their governments are increasingly forced to reduce the direct and indirect costs of labour in their countries and at the same time to offer sweeteners to attract capital investment their way. Deregulation has become the order of the day.

In the industrialised countries governments facing rising welfare payments especially for the new unemployed have begun to meet their bills by making cuts in benefits and by privatising state industries. The net result of this is more inequalities, more wealth for owners of capital and fat cat directors, more unemployed, and poorer wages and conditions for the employed. At the same time, governments with their faith in monetary rewards to encourage investment, have begun to cut the taxes of the rich and increase indirect taxation, which falls proportionately more heavily on the poor. As the incomes of the rich grow and those of the poor decline, ever new innovations are needed to ensure that the rich, old and new, keep up their purchases. 'How to spend it' preoccupies the new consumer society. In the search for markets for the increased output, exports from the industrialised countries grow faster than production.

The case for overcoming inequalities

Although the Blair-Schroeder joint text affirms its pride in the historical achievements of the two parties, there is a great deal of evidence that this pride must be taken with a large pinch of salt. Virtually nothing of the historical achievements of either Party would be unchallenged if the current literal devaluation of their objectives were to be applied retrospectively. In the past, we are told:

> *'The promotion of social justice was sometimes confused with the imposition of equality of outcome. The result was a neglect of the importance of rewarding effort and responsibility, and the association of social democracy with conformity and mediocrity, rather than the celebration of creativity, diversity and excellence. Work was burdened with ever higher costs.'*

But, as we have seen, rewards today do not go through any measures of justice, leave alone mercy or charity. More than ever before, 'it's the rich what gets the pleasure and it's the poor what gets the blame'.

On the question of equality of outcome, we could do better than recall some words of George Bernard Shaw, which are still timely.

> 'Nothing, therefore, is really in question, or ever has been, but the differences between class incomes. Already there is economic equality between captains, and economic equality between cabin boys. What is at issue still is whether there shall be economic equality between captains and cabin boys. What would Jesus have said? Presumably he would have said that if your only object is to produce a captain and a cabin boy for the purpose of transferring you from Liverpool to New York, or to manoeuvre a fleet and carry powder from the magazine to the gun, then you need give no more than a shilling to the cabin boy for every pound you give to the more expensively trained captain. But if in addition to this you desire to allow the two human souls which are inseparable from the captain and the cabin boy and which alone differentiate them from the donkey-engine, to develop all their possibilities, then you may find the cabin boy costing rather more than the captain, because the cabin boy's work does not do so much for the soul as captain's work. Consequently you will have to give him at least as much as the captain unless you definitely wish him to be a lower creature ...'

The case for equality, in other words, is nothing to do with the politics of jealousy, but it is everything to do with removing impediments to the fulfilment of human potential. Today, the difference between the captain and the cabin boy is as nothing compared with the difference between the captain of industry, or the generals of the finance corporations on the one hand, and the victims of modern poverty on the other. Since it is fashionable to praise the global scale of modern industry, let us look at this from a global point of view. To begin with, equality of 'outcome' cannot be properly measured by income alone. What has been largely ignored in this discussion is the distribution of wealth itself.

The United Nations Development Programme, in its **Annual Human Development Reports**, has shown continuous polarisation in property holding.

> 'In 1960 the 20% of the world's people who live in the richest countries had 30 times the income of the poorest 20% – by 1995 82 times as much income.'

But the 225 richest people in the world today have a combined wealth of over one trillion dollars, which is equal to the annual income of the poorest 47% of the world's people. (That is to say, 2.5 billion individuals.) If we look at the gross domestic product of the least developed countries, we find that the combined GDP of 48 countries is less than the wealth of the three richest people in the world. Fifteen billionaires have assets greater than the total national income of Africa south of the Sahara. Thirty-two people own more than the annual income of all the people of South Asia. Eighty-four rich people have holdings greater than the GDP of China, a nation with 1.2 billion citizens. Such figures represent a blight on human development.

The UNDP estimates that the cost of maintaining universal basic education, health care for all, reproductive health care for all women, and adequate food and safe water for all, would be 40 billion dollars a year, or less than 4% of the combined value of the holdings of the 225 richest people. We can be sure of one thing: this polarisation will continue, come hell or high water, come whatever crisis may fall upon us. This year's UNDP Report was starker than last year's, and next year's will be starker than that for this year. Why not raise a 4% tax on precisely these 225 people, and simply meet the outstanding needs identified by the UN? In our present polity, the right to property for some has suffocated all the other rights of many.

Social ownership still vital

It was long ago that socialists and social democrats transferred their focus from the distribution of property to the distribution of income, and so it is much to the credit of the United Nations' development economists that they have helped us to keep the question of property distribution under surveillance. There are as many ways of holding property in common as there are of holding it in private, but what is clear is that the conundrum posed by Bernard Shaw will remain eccentric, even perverse, unless the original social focus that holding property in common comes again to predominate over the discussion of the distribution of income.

The socialisation of enterprise has been the continuing problem in socialist experiments since the beginnings of modern industry. Innumerable efforts to democratise industry have sparked communes, co-operatives, municipal and national public enterprises. There have indeed been long periods in our history when public enterprise has not been a contradiction in terms, even if there have also been socialist crises in which it has. There have been equally long periods when private enterprise has been neither private nor enterprising. But the Third Way is not interested in close scrutiny of these processes. It is entirely content with one of the oldest dogmas of the modern age, which echoes the basic doctrines of laissez-faire in insisting that 'the essential function of markets must be complemented and improved by political action, not hampered by it'.

Much water has gone under the bridge since this modern aphorism was first minted. So at this point in its argument, the Third Way removes its goals from the arena of political economy, and seeks to place them instead in the realm of 'common destiny within the European Union'. Yet every one of these chosen goals lives uneasily with the so-called free market and may at any point conflict with it. 'To promote employment' is not at all necessarily a task for the market, which, left to itself, will with equal or greater force extinguish employment. The market values labour productivity, and cheapness of production, which may quite normally promote prosperity for some few at the expense of jobs for many others.

Where, then, does the market stand in relationship to the 'opportunity to fulfil the unique potential of every individual'? The market enriches some while it impoverishes others, so that it is the true handmaiden of social exclusion, and the driving force behind increasing poverty. For promoters of the Third Way, destiny is a good uplifting word, which indeed lifts our 'values' above the real world, into a stratosphere of high irrelevance and cynicism. But the air up there is very thin, and neither people nor their values can easily survive in it.

Today we see how property and power have been concentrated into the tyranny of a tiny minority, which makes all considerations about equalising incomes to appear positively utopian. The truth is that Governments will not regulate these vast concentrations of wealth, because they dare not. The equivocations of the Joint Declaration only serve to camouflage this reality, which risks putting a full stop to democracy.

Why should this be so? Because the concentration of wealth and power interdicts democratic reform, and the most rudimentary programmes of welfare come under relentless pressure, since even mildly redistributive polices are ruled out of consideration.

The Joint Declaration speaks of 'rewarding effort and responsibility'. These are weasel words. How can the fortunes or the world's 225 most potent billionaires be said to reflect, in any way at all, any kind of personal effort or responsibility? What they reflect is the sway of corporate power.

Huge rewards have been conferred on these individuals, for sure. But they are the misdirected rewards of social effort, individually appropriated. New Labour and *Die Neue Mitte* seek to persuade us that any effort to claw back even a proportion of these ill-gotten gains would undermine creativity, diversity and excellence, and enforce the drear sovereignty of conformity and mediocrity. But the gold standard of mediocrity is surely established by those very politicians who proclaim this doctrine. Their creativity is all bound up with the art of apologetics, while their excellence is defined by their designer wardrobes and the admiration of their peers. Well-turned-out though they evidently are, these emperors have no moral clothes, not a rag of decency between them.

Blocking redistribution by privatisation

Having established its criterion for the redistribution of wealth: hands off!, the declaration then moves over to the offensive against public spending, and the public services.

'The real test for society', it says, 'is how effectively this expenditure is used and how much it enables people to help themselves.'

There are many ways in which public welfare payments can assist in developing self-respect and autonomous action among their beneficiaries. But that is not the direction in which the Third Way leads. On the contrary, it seeks to reduce public spending, and above all to restrain and cut back the bills for public welfare. High among its targets are pensioners, disabled people and others who are, if the truth is told, in a very difficult position when they are invited 'to help themselves'.

In Britain the Welfare Reform Bill seeks to recoup £1.3 billion, mainly from disabled people. In Germany, prodigious onslaughts on the pensioners have been announced. 'We have to grit our teeth' says Mr Schroeder. Accordingly, following Mrs. Thatcher, the SPD now proposes to ditch the upgrading of pensions in line with average wage rates, and to link pension increments only to inflation. Ten billion pounds are to be recouped by these and associated measures. But the British experience shows that over the years, the 'savings' will be very much greater, and the misery very much more extensive, than that. Here again, the Third Way provides a road for the engines of exclusion to accelerate.

Pensioners in both countries have always hitherto been encouraged to believe that pensions were a reward for a lifetime of work and financial contributions. But now the *Neue Mitte* will lead the German people inexorably in the direction of Thatcher's pension regime, which universalises poverty for all those who have already suffered a working lifetime of poverty and low pay. It would, after all, be fearfully bad to encourage our older people to worship the false god of equality of outcome!

These and many other onslaughts on the poor, and the weaker groupings in society, are all justified in the sacred name of the market, which has deposited the problem of poverty at the feet of reluctant Governments, while piling up returns for the 'enterprising', 'creative' wholly 'excellent' nabobs who star as the controllers of all things among the 225 lords of the universe.

So the Declaration tells us:

'The belief that the state should address damaging market failures all too often led to a disproportionate expansion of the Government's reach and the bureaucracy that went with it.'

There is truth in this contention, because, with a certain failure of nerve on the part of social democratic and centrist Governments, public policy moved from ensuring continuing and efficient supplies of certain basic utilities, into rescue operations which were very difficult to sustain. The overnight nationalisation of Rolls Royce by Sir Edward Heath's Government is a perfect case in point. The rescue worked, so that Heath's successors could profitably restore the public corporation to private enterprise. But other rescues by the subsequent Labour Government did not work, whether because of the intrusive intervention of bureaucracy or because of Government inefficiency, or more likely because of the surrounding suffocating chaos in the competitive world of the automobile industry. Public ownership was used to resuscitate these market failures, not to move to more rational pursuit of the public good.

A careful balance sheet of these initiatives would be of considerable interest but it would not prove the case which is made in the Joint Declaration. If public enterprise gave cause for dissatisfaction in Britain, this was frequently because Government policy restricted its operations, controlled and hindered its investment policies, and used its workforce as target guinea-pigs in its regressive wage policies. To be sure, 'individual responsibility and community spirit' sometimes suffered as a result. But what they suffered was discriminatory treatment, because private enterprise tended to avoid such kinds of State interference.

If the Third Way led in any other direction than that of accommodation to a repellent status quo, surely the Joint Declaration would have needed to address the balance sheet of privatisations, most of which had little or no justification beyond free market dogmas. The British public utilities have contributed greatly to the enrichment of their new proprietors, but little to the provision of cheap and efficient services, and less to good environmental practice. The British Railways remain a miserable and dangerous slum service, visibly deteriorating. A coldly exact balance sheet of these social outrages would tell us many things which spokesmen of the Third Way do not wish to know.

But what do they need to know when they tell us that rights have been elevated above responsibilities, and that 'the responsibility of the individual to his or her family, neighbourhood and society cannot be off-loaded on to the state'?

This alleged implosion of responsibility is nominated as the evident cause of rising crime and vandalism, and 'a legal system that cannot cope'. This is a classic reversal of the true chain of causality.

In fact, both sets of phenomena, to the extent that they actually exist, can trace their origins to a common source: the rise and rise of permanent mass unemployment which has ruptured the economic security of whole sections of the population, broken up families and destroyed hope for new generations. In these circumstances, rising crime is an embodiment of the very creativity and enterprise which the Third Way seeks to affirm: although it is, as it always was, in the field of the overall economy, a less than desirable condition. Full employment does not guarantee the achievement of those remaining social goods to which the joint declaration is willing to give its tentative allegiance. But without full employment it is quite certain that crime will prosper, and family breakdown intensify.

But this elementary truth cannot be recognised, because according to the Anglo-German paper 'the ability of national governments to fine tune the economy in order to secure growth and jobs has been exaggerated. The importance of individual and business enterprise to the creation of wealth has been undervalued. The weaknesses of markets have been overstated and their strengths underestimated'.

Market deregulation leads to the Servile State

And here we reach the nub of a very important question. To the extent that the hostile pressures of 'business enterprise' undermine the freedom of Government action, thoughtful socialists had reached the conclusion that joint and combined action involving several governments might be able to accomplish what separate national policies could not. This was the predominant socialist validation of the notion of European Union. Without it, the rationale of European Union completely disappears for all the poorest people, and the preponderant majority of working people. It is true that the strengths of markets have been underestimated, but that is because they are driving forward a polarisation of economic power and democratic impotence which will ensure that the Third Way leads us ever more surely into arbitrary government and economic serfdom.

Markets have been opened up everywhere to the free movement of goods and of capital. The result of freeing trade in manufactured goods under successive rounds of GATT negotiations was enormously to strengthen the position of the already industrialised countries against whose products the infant industries of the newly industrialising countries could not hope to compete. Only powerful state support and protection against imports allowed the East Asian tigers to capture a place in the world markets for manufactured goods. For all their fine talk about free trade, governments of the industrialised countries continued to use every kind of subsidy and protective device to support their own favoured industries, especially the arms industry. Agricultural production in particular continued to be heavily protected, which further weakened the position of the non-industrialised countries, whose farmers could not hope to compete with the industrialised countries' subsidised grains and other substitutes for their tropical products.

Now, the freeing of capital movements has had even more disastrous results in generating inequalities. Capital moves mainly between the already industrialised countries, encouraging each to offer subsidies and tax rebates as inducements. These are of course paid for by the ordinary tax-payer for the benefit of the capital investor, and possibly if the investment is viable for the workforce employed. At the same time a stream of funds began to flow into the newly industrialising countries, first in Latin America and then in East Asia and finally into Russia and Eastern Europe, in expectation of high returns, especially in property development. When these hopes collapsed, there were heavy losses, especially for the small investors but much of the big companies' money simply flowed back. This was enough, however, in 1998 to cause a major global crisis as speculative investment in the newly industrialising economies failed. Even the great Japanese economy went into reverse and massive sums of national and international finance were made available to rescue failing finance houses in the USA and bankrupt governments in Latin America and in Russia.

Surplus capital has become a world-wide phenomenon, even while larger and larger numbers of men and women fall into poverty. In earlier periods of such capital accumulation in the long cycles of boom and slump, the crisis was severe enough and the slumps deep enough, or great wars intervened, to effect what was called the 'creative destruction' of capital assets. No one dares to contemplate a major war, with nuclear weapons, but minor wars in Iraq and Yugoslavia will have created the need for some replacement of buildings, bridges and plant and, of course, weapons. In recent years, a deep slump has been averted by government intervention, but the accumulation of wealth at one pole and poverty at the other is the classic and continuing prescription for breakdown.

The case for reduced public spending deeply flawed

'Ideas of what is left wing should never become an ideological straight-jacket.'

What the Declaration is telling us is that the people who are being pulverised in the convulsions of economic change need unprincipled politicians to serve them. They need spokesmen who will 'create the conditions in which existing businesses can prosper and adapt'. It appears that they have found just such paragons in those who conduct the affairs of the present SPD and the British Labour Party. What programmes do they propose?

New technologies change the nature of work, and result in the simultaneous de-skilling and dismissal of some people, but, we are told, they also 'create new business and vocational opportunities'. This question has been discussed *ad nauseam*, for thirty years or more. But it has become increasingly evident that the renewal process is much slower than the demolition of employment. This fact correlates with two others, which socialists should examine, and on which there should be informed debate.

Firstly, higher unemployment is linked to increasingly wide disparities in the distribution of wealth and resources. The 200-odd billionaires who dominate the world economy will soon shrink in numbers to 150 or fewer, each of them richer than ever before, while unemployment rises to a yet higher plateau. Secondly, the paralysis of states has meant that effective counteraction has become increasingly uncommon. More public enterprise, more intervention, more activism by Governments is a necessary response to a capitalism whose dynamism has become increasingly and evidently self-destructive. As always, it makes the rich richer and the poor poorer. But now it damages the fabric of social reproduction more wantonly than ever before. In this work of destruction, governments of the Third Way can play a very major role indeed. Moving from the macro-economic level to the micro, the Declaration tells us 'having the same job for life is a thing of the past'. Somebody took up this thought some years ago at a seminar, and has been recycling it down the Third Way for all it's worth. Thus it has been repeated very many times. But it is not true. As we have seen in the ILO **Report on World Employment 1996/97**, the evidence for this proposition was examined. The data shows something quite different: that 'there is hardly any universal trend towards increased instability among major industrialised nations …'. Those presently employed have been in their jobs, on average, between six and twelve years, dependent on the country in which they have been working: 'and this figure has not been declining'.

On the environment, the Declaration does recognise 'an increasing challenge in reconciling environmental responsibility towards future generations with material progress for society at large'. This recognition entails, we are told, a marriage between such a responsibility and a market-based approach. No doubt such an approach will emerge in the continuous dialogues between Government Ministers and representatives of Monsanto or Novartis, who are pressing ahead to develop genetically modified crops. Maybe the social gain of this process may be measured in the donations of these entrepreneurs to the Labour Party, which may partly replace the fall in its subscriptions, as Party members defect in droves.

Public expenditure has more or less reached the limits of its acceptability, the Declaration continues. But where are these limits to be found? Tax takes and public spending vary between the different advanced states: who gives us our model?

Taking taxes and social security contributions together, as a percentage of gross domestic product, we find wide variations across the European Union (see Table 1). The combined totals in Germany run at 37.5%, and in the UK at 35.3%. But Sweden commits 53.3% of its GDP, and Finland 47.3%. Belgium and France

Table 1:
Government Receipts from Taxes and Social Security Contributions as a percentage of GDP (market prices), 1986 and 1997 (in order of size in 1997 for EU countries)

Country	1997		1986	
	Order	%	Order	%
Sweden	1	53.3	1	52.5
Finland	2	47.3	=7	42.4
Belgium	3	46.5	2	46.3
France	4	46.1	=5	44.0
Luxembourg	5	45.6	=5	44.0
Italy	6	44.9	12	36.0
Austria	7	44.4	=7	42.4
Netherlands	8	43.4	4	44.9
Norway	9	42.5	3	45.5
Germany	10	37.5	10	37.7
Spain	=11	35.3	13	30.4
UK	=11	35.3	9	37.8
Ireland	13	34.8	·11	37.2
Portugal	14	34.5	14	33.6
Iceland	15	32.0	15	28.4
Australia		30.3		30.8
Canada		na		33.8
Czech Republic		39.4		na
Japan		na		28.4
Switzerland		34.6		31.9
USA		na		25.8

*Source: ONS **Economic Trends**, London, March 1999, pp. 51-2*

each raise more than 46% of their GDP from taxes and social security payments. Italy and Austria come just over one per cent lower at 44.9% and 44.4%. It is perfectly true that the United States (at the last available figure of 32%) and Japan (at 28.4%) run at a lower level. But what are the 'limits of acceptability'? They appear to be almost twice as high in Sweden as they are in Japan, while Britain and Germany both lag far behind smaller EU countries which commit considerably larger proportions of their resources.

Who has measured the acceptable limits of public expenditure? And by what means? The extent of variations, country by country, appears to be so wide as to permit much scope for experimentation. But the Third Way offers us 'constraints on "tax and spend".' These constraints are presented as if they were immutable economic laws, when all the evidence shows that they are not. They are concessions to monetarist fashion, which runs high in Britain, because of the exemplary influence of the United States. Not to put too fine a point on it, such constraint is founded solely on monetarist dogma. And yet, still as a fundamental law of the economy, we are presented with the need for 'radical modernisation of the public sector, and reform of public services to achieve better value for money.'

In this way, we are bamboozled to accept private finance initiatives (PFI) which are mortgages on the capital investments of health and education services. Private developers build hospitals and lease them to the Health Service in Britain, for a fixed and profitable period of time. The expiry of the lease leaves the facilities in question in the ownership of the original investors. Meantime public services have paid continuously high rents out of their annual appropriations, thus diminishing the resources which would otherwise be available for treatment in hospitals or for pedagogy in schools. Direct public borrowing would be far cheaper than these rack-renting mortgages, but in Britain, under the archaic methods of accounting imposed by the Treasury to control the Public Sector Borrowing Requirement, public borrowing is outlawed, while far more expensive private borrowing is not. So elastic are these 'limits of acceptability'!

This corrupt generation of politicians has inherited very high public investment in hospitals, universities and schools, made by the postwar generations which suffered the incidence of high levels of taxation with very little complaint. Now tax rates are far lower, and prejudice dictates that they may not be raised. Instead, the PFI off-loads the social costs of health and educational investment on to future generations, in a cynical mortgage which buys political power by lowering our own taxes so that our children's will rise. 'After us, the deluge ...'

Already the social costs of this policy are reflected in 'ever more pressing problems of crime, social disintegration and drug abuse'. Social democrats 'need to find ways of combating' these.

It is of course very popular to insist that crime should be repressed, because it is an increasing scourge for large numbers of people, often themselves needy and ill-able to cope with its results. But much crime results directly from mass unemployment, especially youth unemployment. The introduction of workfare schemes provides only partial relief, and at the same time builds new forms of alienation which are all-too-likely themselves to exacerbate the problem of crime. Crime and poverty live close together, and the Third Way recognises especially the problem of family poverty.

'We need specific measures for those who are most threatened by marginalisation'. But the force which is driving increased marginalisation, increased unemployment, and greatly increased social exclusion, is the market. The success of the market in generating that competition which is supposed to lead to growth, must be measured in the inequalities which result.

We are told that modern social democrats appreciate the doctrine of subsidiarity and seek to solve problems where they can best be solved. *'As a general principle, power should be devolved to the lowest possible level'*. But the market actually concentrates power, and has given us a world in which our famous 225 billionaires own more than a trillion dollars, while 2.5 billions of people own nearly nothing. This is a triumph of the entrepreneurial spirit, and Third Way social democrats seek to correct it by … promoting entrepreneurial spirit. Far from taxing the 225, and sharing their obscene holdings to promote initiative among the masses, the Third Way exists to 'celebrate' successful entrepreneurs. These celebrations entail the rekindling of community and solidarity, not among the victims, the deprived people of the world, but between 'all groups in society'. Solidarity with the Sultan of Brunei is the preferred option: perhaps he will reward those who speak out for it? Solidarity with Sultans is a by-word in Britain which pioneered this far-sighted social policy. But the Joint Declaration tells us to be of good heart, because similar solidarity is now breaking out in Germany itself, 'with employees having the opportunity of sharing the rewards of success with employers'. That is to say, employees are encouraged to applaud the enterprise of those employers who have far-sightedly exported their jobs to the East, in order to maximise profit and unemployment at the same time.

How the new supply-side agenda undermines social standards

In recognising that unemployment is far too high in Europe, the proponents of the Third Way call for a new supply-side agenda for the left. This has been called for before the Blair era, and long before the destruction of the agenda for real employment, which has been developed in Germany by Oskar Lafontaine. The Third Way avoids any serious discussion of the proposals of Jacques Delors, who has become as much of an unperson as the old Soviet leaders who preceded Stalin and were all airbrushed out of the photographs in the history books. What are the ingredients of this supply-side agenda?

Firstly, 'a robust and competitive market framework'. Secondly, a growth-oriented tax policy. Thirdly, flexibility in product, capital and labour markets, by removing the rules and regulations which inhibit our gifted entrepreneurs.

An orgy of flexibility is prescribed, allowing Europe a chance to catch up with the United States. Thus 'millions of our people' will gain the chance to find new jobs, learn new skills, pursue new careers, set up and expand new businesses. In non-Third Way speak, this means that millions of people are expected to lose their present jobs, and to find new ones. Some of these, but not many, will be more advanced than their present occupations and they will need somehow to obtain the new knowledge and skill updates which will allow them to survive. Others will simply be worse. All these new jobs will not be regulated in the way that the old jobs were. Regulation would only slow down the process of innovation. In this way, millions of people will be liberated from economic security and the old bad habits of a protected social environment. Perhaps the Third Way may also liberate them from social democracy as well.

This part of the Blair/Schroeder agenda is recycled from another Joint Declaration, proclaimed by Blair with the Spanish Prime Minister Jose Aznar. This caused some wry responses by Social Democratic Governments in other European countries, because Blair had deliberately sought a political marriage with the centre right Prime Minister of Spain, rather than any of his other potential (Social Democratic) partners elsewhere in Europe. They, of course, were less spontaneously ready for the gospel of deregulation than was the Spanish leader. But the Blair/Aznar document itself was not exactly new. All of its detailed proposals are to be found in the 1993 Green Paper on **Growth, Competitiveness and Employment in the European Community**, prepared by the Major Government and submitted during the consultations organised by the European Commission, in connection with the launching of the Delors White Paper on these matters.

In spite of the massive proliferation of research staff in Blair's *cabinet*, it is evidently easier to copy out yesterday's official proclamations than to originate new ones for tomorrow. The advantage of this process is that, over a period of a few months, it has been possible to realign a British Labour Government **and** a German Social Democratic coalition, with the Spanish Conservatives, in a drive to cut out regulations which are thought to jeopardise competitiveness.

'We will not support measures leading to a higher tax burden' says the Anglo-German statement. Soon afterwards it was announced that public spending in Britain had reached a new postwar low, while poverty and its attendant problems continue to weigh heavier than ever on the British polity.

Growing inequalities reduce economic performance

Even short of a major crisis of 1929 proportions, the effects of growing inequality are likely to be serious both politically and economically. The widening gap between the conspicuous consumption of the rich and the increasing impoverishment of large numbers of their fellow citizens can only lead to theft and mugging, to more organised crime and a general breakdown of law and order. If governments will not redistribute income, other ways will be found. The numbers of police increase, prisons overflow and Neighbourhood

Watch grows into guarded and defended fortresses for the wealthy. Government 'cohesion units' and Inner City task forces can deal only with the symptoms and not the causes of the trouble.

Abandonment of Keynesian prescriptions for full employment has also involved neglect of Keynes's warnings: not only that unregulated capitalism tends to generate increasing disparities of wealth, but that great inequality of income would undermine economic performance. Keynes believed, as New Labour evidently does, that 'there are valuable human activities which require the motive of money-making and the environment of private wealth ownership for their full fruition.' While, however, he believed that 'there is social and psychological justification for significant inequalities of income and wealth', he added, 'but not for such large disparities as exist today.' (*General Theory* p. 374)

The basis for Keynes's argument that the disparities were too large was the effect of such disparities on aggregate national (or international) purchasing power. Investment in the economy, on his argument, does not depend upon adequate savings but upon an adequate propensity to consume. The rich save more of their incomes; the poor consume more. Government demand can keep up aggregate demand – through its consumption and investment. But government demand depends on government taxing or borrowing (within limits) and on government spending. This is the famous (or infamous) 'tax and spend' which New Labour believes to be both obsolete and perverse, but which many economists regard as necessary for economic growth and full employment. The alternative policies being offered by governments today of raising or lowering interest rates to discourage or encourage economic activity may well provide some discouragement but are not enough in themselves to encourage economic activity even with some aid to improve the supply of labour and capital.

For full employment of resources some action on the demand side was regarded as essential by Keynes and all those who had learnt the lessons of the 1930s slump.

To quote Keynes again: 'For, if effective demand is deficient, not only is the public scandal of wasted resources intolerable, but the individual enterpriser who seeks to bring these resources into action is operating with the odds loaded against him.'

Support for Keynes's views is said by all those who today reject old Labour policies to be lacking, but the distinguished British Clare Group of economists has argued that

> 'The surge of investment was the significant influence on the high tide of full employment in the 1950s and 1960s ... What were the conditions that induced the surge of investment?...The first was the confidence engendered by the full employment policy itself ... the second was that the government set out to encourage it by all manner of special incentives.'
> (National Institute *Economic Review*, February, 1995)

The UNDP Report for 1997, moreover, showed that world-wide inequalities are greatest inside the poorest countries and argued that a reduction in poverty and the establishment of greater equality encourages growth – through better health and more education and generally greater preparedness to take risks and engage in new enterprise. The International Labour Office has added its voice, representative of governments, employers and trade unions, arguing that

> 'The pace of globalisation has been primarily driven by market forces, and national and to some extent international rules, institutions and practices needed to render its consequences socially acceptable have been insufficiently developed.'
> (ILO, *World Labour Report 1998-9*)

Neglect of social concerns is not just a matter of an immoral extent of social exclusion, but in widening the gap between rich and poor and weakening the power of labour, it reduces the whole performance of the economy

> 'Ironically, there has been a very close correlation between the extent to which capital has got its way and the extent to which the performance of the advanced capitalist economies has deteriorated cycle by cycle, since the 1980s. During the 1960s, when ostensibly over-strong labour movements, bloated welfare states, and hyper-regulating governments were at the height of their influence, the global economic boom reached historic peaks. Since then, as the neo-classical medicine has been administered in ever stronger doses, the economy has performed less well.'
> (Robert Brenner, 'The Economics of Global Turbulence: A Special Report on the World Economy, 1950-98', *New Left Review*, May-June, 1998)

The power of the state

An end to such medication and a return to more egalitarian policies imply a reinforcement of state intervention in the economy. It is sometimes said that the power of the state has been superseded by the power of the giant accumulators of capital. This is not true: what has happened is that the state has become the host for the transnational economy. It is more than ever required to sustain that accumulation by regulatory and redistributive measures, but in the interest of capital, not labour. At the same time, the resources of states have been definitely weakened, partly by deliberate action – the reduction of taxes on personal and corporate wealth – partly by tax avoidance and indeed tax evasion. Not only have the transnationally operating companies used transfer pricing to declare profits only where taxation is minimal or nil, in tax havens like the Bahamas and Lichtenstein, but wealthy individuals are increasingly placing their money in such tax havens – the Channel Islands and the Isle of Man being the preferred locations for British funds. It is said that Mr Murdoch and his companies have paid no UK taxes for several years.

We are not talking about small sums. Such funds owned by British citizens in tax havens are estimated to be equal to the whole UK gross annual national product, about £400 billion. Wealthy Germans have parked 200 billion marks (£70 billion) just in Luxemburg alone. The IMF estimates very conservatively that the total sums managed under the flag of various off-shore states is of the order of $2000 billion. Where then is all this money invested by the financial institutions that manage such vast funds? It is clearly not spent on consumption which might create employment. It is not held in savings accounts. It is in part invested in company shares, pushing up share prices to heights quite unjustified by the real assets of the companies, and most riskily supported, because the rich believe that they can always borrow to buy because share values are rising. Increasingly the greater part of the surplus capital is invested speculatively in the money markets, including the foreign exchange markets. Felix Rohatyn, a leading New York banker, has declared that 'the world finance markets are today a greater danger to stability than atomic weapons.'

One of the main finance markets is the market in foreign exchange. The billions of dollars, pounds, marks, franks and yen that are exchanged in these markets every working day are not used for foreign travel or even for foreign trade and long term investment. By far the greater part is involved in speculation on anticipated changes in currency values. This might be no more than the froth on the top of the natural flow of moneys in international transactions, but it has a much more damaging effect. All the speculation places national currencies in an international pecking order according to the confidence that the market operators have in the currencies continuing at their current value or improving on it for reasons that have to do with what is regarded as sound finance – open markets for money and goods, but no foreign payments deficits, and especially low inflation and well controlled government spending. These are the matters to which the power of the state is expected to be directed.

Any action by governments to regulate the international movement of money or goods, or to redistribute incomes away from the rich and in favour of the poor, such as might offend the principles of sound finance, will immediately be penalised by sales of that country's currency, leading to its loss of value and to capital flight. At the same time, deliberate devaluing of its currency by a government in order to increase the competitiveness of its products will be met with destablising currency speculation. An intended small adjustment may easily result in a major collapse as automatic computer adjustments are triggered all round the world . Once market confidence in a currency has been lost, it is very hard to re-establish it. Speculation and all short term capital investment tends to follow the multitude. As Keynes insisted, the sum of individual actors responding to rational incentives does not at all necessarily result in the optimum use of resources. Just as it is with companies, which each might contract employment to restore profitability, the consequence is to reduce aggregate demand and weaken the whole economy, so is it with separate nation states following deflationary policies.

What can be done nationally and internationally
While individual nation state governments, except for the United States, can do little on their own to resist the giant companies, an association of states like the European Union could do much. For a time, it seemed as if the European Union might take actions both to resist the dominant position of United States capital and jointly to return their economies to full employment. This now appears

unlikely. The US hegemony is not to be challenged, nor any harmonisation of policies achieved. The new social democratic governments of Germany, France and Italy as well as the Scandinavians have turned their backs on such possibilities and joined New Labour in following what is called the Third Way, but we have seen to be in effect a continuation of the unregulated capitalist policies of previous right-wing governments.

Some things can still be done both nationally and internationally. The struggle to defend the welfare state can be most effectively advanced by combination of national actions with European-wide links. In place of the current downward pressure on best European practice to reduce all to a common low level, a process of upward harmonisation could be called for. Information about best practice in the several countries of the European Union could be widely publicised as the basis for campaigns by the special interest groups – pensioners, unemployed, the sick and disabled, parents of young children and especially single parents. The need is to find ways of bringing together these groups in national and European wide alliances to challenge the backward drift represented by the Blair-Schroeder manifesto. Already, there have been major protest movements against the cuts in social provision being proposed in France and Germany and Italy. In the UK, where such provision is among the very lowest to be found in all Europe, resistance to further reductions has been growing in spite of the complicity of New Labour.

Wider international action has not been lacking. The movement of protest at the failure of governments to forgive the debts of the poorest countries has forced this issue onto the agenda of the rich countries' governments. Protests by non-governmental organisations at proposals for a Multi-national Agreement on Investment (MAI) that would open up all countries to free movements of capital has been successful in preventing its introduction. A major campaign is now needed to introduce some curbs on capital speculation. Professor Tobin, a Nobel prize-winning economist, has proposed a tax on all speculative transactions – a proposal which Keynes had already considered in 1930 in his *Treatise on Money*. There is a very wide body of public opinion that is worried about the environmental effects of deregulation on the food we eat, the air we breathe and the water we drink. Vague phrases about responsibility for the environment are no substitute for rules and regulations which are pilloried in the Blair-Schroeder document as only so many 'gags' on the new opportunities for business.

New Labour: serving the public or the Servile State?

Governments which serve the interests of capital appear to believe that, with the dissolution of a potential Soviet alternative, there are no limits to the extent that they may go in protecting those interests. It is for labour to show now that these limits have been far exceeded and it is time for a return to the middle way of Keynes, who wrote that 'the Republic of my imagination lies on the extreme left of celestial space'; while remembering, as Skidelsky comments, that 'the ideal he sometimes chose to call socialist has much more to do with ends such as leisure, beauty, grace, excitement, variety ... than with equality, fraternity, democracy.'

Nonetheless, in a note on 'post war employment' written in 1944 for the Treasury Post-War Steering Committee, Keynes wrote

> 'it will be the role of this country to develop a middle way of economic life which will preserve the liberty, the initiative and (what we are so rich in) the idiosyncrasy of the individual in a framework serving the public good and seeking equality of contentment amongst all.'
> (quoted as the epigraph for Jonathan Kirshner's article on 'Keynes, capital mobility and the crisis of embedded liberalism' in *Review of International Political Economy*, Autumn, 1999)

It is this framework that is being destroyed by the proponents of the New Middle. If it cannot be rebuilt, then even more profound changes will become necessary, and sooner than is generally understood.

The future, in both Germany and Britain, will be bleak indeed, if the Third Way marks out the real choices which have been made by their leaders.

> 'Companies must have room for manoeuvre to take advantage of important economic conditions and seize new opportunities: they must not be gagged by rules and regulations.
> 'Product, capital and labour markets must all be flexible. We must not combine rigidity in one part of the economic system with openness and dynamism in the rest.'

The Servile State: New Labour, new servility

After a bonfire of the regulations, with social protections going up in smoke, we can arrive at 'an active labour market policy for the left'. There was a time when socialists insisted that the labour market as a whole was a major criticism of the rule of capital. 'Workers are not things' we used to think. Alienation was a condition in which 'things are in the saddle and ride mankind'. A socialist polity would be one in which labour employed capital, not capital, labour. In this way, the capital market would be at the service of associated labourers. But now, the highest dream of the Third Way is that the invisible hand will advance the interests of capital by pulling down yesterday's restrictions on the 'flexibility' of labour, yesterday's protections of humanity, while the invisible foot kicks recalcitrants into line. New Labour, new servility!

Schroeder and Blair provide us with a perfect map of the servile state, in which Government exists only as the handmaiden of capital. It is in this spirit that *die Neue Mitte* promises

> 'We will establish a network of experts, far-sighted thinkers, political fora and discussion meetings. We will thereby deepen and continually further develop the concept of the new centre and the Third Way. This is the priority for us'.

In this way, the wheel has turned full circle. For these leaders, socialism is now permanent counter-revolution. With the labour market ever-more deregulated, the labourer ever-more subordinated to commercial logic, government ever-more prostituted in the service of business, the larger the better, we are arriving in that Orwellian Kingdom where freedom is slavery, and all can truly, at last, love Big Brother.

And yet, to echo Oskar Lafontaine, the heart still beats on the left, and it is among the little brothers and sisters that hope will survive, and ultimately triumph.

Justice is Timely

Twelve theses for a modern socialist policy. A necessary response to Gerhard Schroeder and Tony Blair.

Gregor Gysi

Dr Gysi is the leader of the Party of Democratic Socialism (PDS) in Germany.

In almost all the countries of the European Union, forces representing democratic socialism influence policies through opposition, tolerance and participation in government. But an analysis of neo-conservative strategy, as well as social democracy, is needed. Common ground must be staked out, and differences highlighted. The ideas of a modern socialist Left have to be spelt out in order to win support.

Free development of the individual as the prerequisite for the free development of all – that is the message of a free, modern and democratic socialism. The political challenge to democratic socialism is to organise society in a way that ensures social and political human rights for one and all. In this sense, socialism is the human rights perspective of modern societies. It calls for equality in freedom, and is based on self-determination and solidarity.

Below are twelve theses for a democratic and socialist policy at the end of the century.

1. The 21st century vision:
combine modernity with socialism

Modern societies are distinct from traditional pre-capitalist, or early capitalist, societies because of 'the permanent transformation of production and the uninterrupted disruption of conditions in society, the eternal insecurity and motion' (Karl Marx). The driving force behind these continuous innovating changes is an institutionalised competition in the economy, politics, science, education, the media and culture, which is based on a pluralistic distribution of property, power and influence. The security of being able to rely on seemingly invariable living conditions throughout life has vanished.

Permanent modernisation is an ambivalent process. During this century, its institutions in the economy, politics, science, education, the media and culture have often been used as the instruments of the fiercest oppression. The disasters of this century, the world wars, the Holocaust, genocide, misery, starvation and environmental destruction, arose from them.

The state socialist attempt to evade the unpredictability and insecurity of capitalism, by replacing competition and evolution with planned control and centralised administration of resources, has failed. Even though, in a historical context, the permanent attempts to defeat state socialism and the conditions resulting from that must be taken into account, one fact remains: the general conditions for innovation and progress were either destroyed or could not emerge. Social security, therefore, did not have a lasting economic basis. Freedom and individual initiative were limited, and fundamental democratic rights were not guaranteed. State socialism resulted in a stagnating society which crumbled and, eventually, collapsed. Nevertheless, it gave humankind an important experience which needs critical analysis, not denunciation.

Socialist policy following the collapse of state socialism should liberate and protect the evolutionary potentials of competition in the economy, politics, science, education, the media and culture from the dominance of capital and its authoritarianism. Only this will make it possible to use competition as a resource for the emancipation and development of all individuals, and to control and compensate in solidarity for the risks, uncertainties and insecurities entailed. The equality of the sexes consequently arises from such a change and is also the prerequisite for its taking place. Embarking on the road to socialist modernity means aiming at the replacement of capital's dominance over the direction, manifestation and speed of change in human civilisation, with the dominance of social, cultural and ecological objectives. To this end, politics must be directed, deliberate efforts made to mould society, and counter-powers developed that are able to bring all this about.

What matters is not the abolition of markets, but the creation of new ones; not the suppression of entrepreneurial initiative, but the creation of new overall conditions for its social and ecological orientation. That cannot be achieved through supplicatory formulae such as those in Schroeder's and Blair's joint proposal, but by limiting the right of disposal of capital and property where it works contrary to the common good, and where it leads to ecological degradation and social disintegration. Public property must assume a new role.

What is intended here is not a relapse into pre-modernity or anti-modernity, but a transformation of modernity. A combination of modernity and socialism is not inevitable. However, it could be the major task for the next generation.

2. Social Democracy in the age of Fordism was rather successful. It can no longer be copied today, but it holds lessons.
Gerhard Schroeder and Tony Blair paint a picture of social democratic policy during the past decades as a source of levelling, phobia towards innovation, permanently increasing public spending put to unproductive uses, étatism, and irresponsibly high material expectations. This picture is unhistorical and unjust. It makes one forget the degree to which productivity and innovation have

developed over the past 50 years, and especially the great influence of social democratic visions on broad sectors of people.

The Fordist welfare state emerging in Western Europe and the US after World War Two was able to guarantee nearly full employment over a lengthy period of prosperity, growing earnings in keeping with the development of productivity, and index-linked social benefits in old age, sickness, disability or unemployment. But poverty has never really been abolished. Industrial mass production of material goods and private mass consumption were prominent features of Fordism. More scope for individual involvement, such as co-determination in companies, and better chances for emancipation were also combined with it. Not all, but quite a few, dreams of the Social Democrats came true. Not only, but mainly, thanks to the trades unions, social democracy, socialist movements and parties, as well as the competition with state socialism, institutions emerged which were able to voice the interests of the working class, and partially to complement capital's leading role in society with social participation. Unfortunately, prosperity was paid for by the oppression and exploitation of the so-called Third World, and an increasing destruction of the natural resources, which have been the means of livelihood for the human species. Yet there has been development here, too. The colonial age is over. These days, the impoverishment and exploitation of the Third World happens through bilateral and international political and economic dependency. Ecology has become a political subject, and a matter of public awareness.

The achievements of state intervention in the market economy are porous and disintegrative. This is not because rapidly growing wages, increasing state redistribution, Keynesian spending policies, and state control over the major players have always been wrong. The limits of the old ideal have to a large degree resulted from its success. The crisis of the Fordist working society results from a type of growth that only worked as long as ever new areas of human life could be turned into gainful employment, organised along economic lines and rationalised until less and less social labour was necessary for the production of the goods needed for consumption and investment. The wealth of free time gained this way in a Fordist working society can only be used to produce and consume more, and it is being invested to save more living labour. This cannot go on without restrictions. The ecological problems generated by this type of growth, and the increase in 'superfluous labour', are manifested in growing discrepancies between capital utilisation, wages, taxes, social surcharges and transfer incomes.

Nowadays, we have reached a point where we need redefinition of the relationship between working and living. Redundant labour cannot be completely reinvested, but it must not become superfluous time, dead time of a seemingly superfluous underclass. And it is just as anachronistic to turn the time available now into cheap, subsidised service jobs. This is the way to a different, new class society – on the one hand the big-income earners with too much work and too little time, and the small-income earners who, as servants, raise the children of the big-income earners, take care of their houses and gardens, and see to all the unprofitable errands. This new split into classes would be anti-modern and anachronistic.

Instead of snorting at the achievements of the social democratic age, as Schroeder and Blair do, efforts should be made to completely revamp and integrate the achievements into new societal structures. A genuine modernisation does not mean dismantling and deregulating social institutions, it means searching for a new path of development and deciding in favour of an alternative reform policy, linking economic, social, ecological and individual developments.

3. The era of neo-liberal destruction of the post-war system should not be merely interrupted by a social democratic episode of damage-containment, but superseded by an episode of modern socialist politics.

Through a chain of aggressive reforms, neo-liberalism has started to dismantle Fordist welfare capitalism over the past twenty years. This was carried out mainly in the interest of transnational corporations and international financial markets, the global economic, political and cultural upper classes. The quest for a new, future-capable way of combining economic development and social progress is not a relevant component of the neo-liberal reform programme. The emergent system is, therefore, extremely unjust, unstable and threatens peace, the environment and social cohesion.

So far, the neo-liberal reforms have been implemented in Germany only in part. Important structural elements of the social democratic era remain intact. These can hamper reform, on the one hand, because justified social interests are represented in an obsolete fashion. On the other hand, they may facilitate reform: there is a chance to transform the existing welfare state and corporate institutions for the new tasks ahead.

Social democracy of the New Centre or the Third Way attempts to pick up on the neo-liberal approach and partially correct it. It tries to give the state a bigger role again, not acting as the Fordist redistributive state, but as an 'activating' force. Like neo-liberalism, it means to establish, promote and moderate market mechanisms and forms of competition which improve the competitiveness of nation-states and major regions in global competition, while (in contrast to Thatcher's neo-liberalism) safeguarding a minimum social consensus at home by promoting the bargaining processes of opponents (such as the Alliance for Jobs in Germany).

The fact that social democratic governments are in office in many European countries proves that the people wanted a correction of the neo-liberal reform strategy. However, the defeat that the German and British Social Democrats suffered in the European elections is a clear sign that their current policy cannot count on stable support. On the one hand, it is unable to take the offensive and make use of new chances. On the other, it has not proved that it can and will effectively oppose new social threats. Hence, it seems equally to step back to pre-neo-liberalism and pre-social democratic times, disappointing both those who have pinned their hopes on new chances and those who are threatened.

4. Those who want to make use of the new chance have to let everybody have an opportunity. Those who want to oppose the new threat must not allow them to attack those who are most vulnerable. Society requires a new consensus.
Social justice is the fundamental social condition for a lasting, truly modern policy. It must not be reduced to individual fairness. The social foundations of individual performance must not be ignored. Democratic socialism, therefore, favours a new consensus in society.

Basic elements of this consensus are:
- a policy that credibly faces the new challenge – turning new chances into chances for a freer development of all, in solidarity;
- a transition to a mode of development that ensures a more just participation of everyone in social wealth through a new way of working and living that is ecologically sustainable;
- surmounting all obstacles in the way of women's self-determination and the equality of the sexes;
- full employment by exploring new fields for economic development in keeping with sustainable, ecological and social criteria, while at the same time reducing hours and increasing the flexibility and enrichment of gainful employment, and its combination with the chance to do voluntary and creative work;
- a social system where costs are shared in solidarity, which aims at basic safeguards for everyone, and the active involvement of all in terms of new opportunities;
- a policy of restructuring public finances, thereby opening the way to a more just social system and new development.

5. Modernising politics means more than adapting to new conditions and supporting business. Above all, politics should be a deliberate effort to structure social conditions. To this end, organised counter-forces are required.
Neo-liberalism turned the politics of nation-states and international organisations into the executive bodies of transnational corporations and international financial markets, to which the framework of Keynesian control over the economy has become captive.

According to Schroeder and Blair, the new social democracy will promote the economy and create overall conditions under which an unhampered functioning of market forces is possible.

Social justice and ecological sustainability are strangers to an unhampered functioning of highly empowered world markets. Expecting social and ecological sustainability from an improvement of the supply situation amongst the current players in these markets would, therefore, either be unworldly or a deliberate ideological hoax. Without strong socially and ecologically oriented forces in society, and global and regional regulation, any change of direction would be impossible.

For democratic socialism, a modernisation of politics cannot mean serving the economy more efficiently and disposing of its unwanted 'waste' in a more social manner. And it is not enough to improve the productive capacity of labour by better training. In the first place, a modernisation of politics means regaining politics as a means of deliberately moulding social conditions to give the forces of the market and society as a whole an orientation towards the common good.

What is needed is a policy of dialogue and a European employment pact. Yet, they only make sense if they open up new chances for those who are unemployed today or are underpaid. The orientation towards the common good requires that those who are disadvantaged today are the ones who benefit. This orientation can only be successful if a higher portion of the gainfully employed share in the national wealth, and small and medium scale entrepreneurs receive support in real terms so that their almost complete dependence on banks and major corporations is clearly reduced.

Political power depends tremendously on the balance of forces in society and, above all, on the economy. Just as a division of powers is the condition for democracy in a political system, a division of economic power is the prerequisite for a social and ecological economic order. Developments oriented towards the common good can only emerge from an institutionalisation of ecological and social counter-forces, in contrast to the power of mere capital utilisation and the misconceptions of maximum wages and consumption.

Those without power are in no position to negotiate, and are not accepted as partners. Organised capital's omnipotence inevitably results in a powerlessness of politics *vis-à-vis* the economy. What are called practical constraints are those constraints that arise from the predominance of the former, and the relative powerlessness of the latter, in the first place. Without a change in the power structures in the economy the 'Alliance for jobs, vocational training and competitiveness' will become a coercive contract providing the biggest companies with the most favours. This will result in social decline, and some social concessions granted rather as an act of grace and favour.

For decades, Social Democrats have failed to prepare people for the fact that road blocks to development can be removed by nothing other than their own involvement in changing the relations of power. It's not by accident that the calls by Gerhard Schroeder and Tony Blair for The Third Way and *die Neue Mitte* (The New Centre) are appeals to the governments, and not the peoples, of Europe.

The emergence towards social and ecological sustainability starts when those affected recognise their own interests. It is based on the commitment to such a change amongst citizens' initiatives, project organisers, associations, trades unions, churches, expert groups and local actors. A modern Left must promote self-organisation and representation of the interests of civil society, contribute to networking, and provide a political framework for initiatives in the quest for a new path of development. The state and legal system gain in importance as they make such developments possible, and promote them by setting the rules.

6. A combination of ecological restructuring, modernisation of working society and the establishment of a multifaceted and varied way of life could create a sustainable type of development which surmounts the obstacles of Fordist capitalism, becomes less harmful to the environment, and facilitates the economic conditions for a freer development of all. What matters is a path of development which supersedes the socially tamed post-war capitalism.

Technologically, societies today are able to supply the needs of everybody on earth with only a small expenditure of labour. However, this development has not led to us all working less. Growing numbers of people capable of gainful employment have no paid job. Others work more and more, and tend to earn more, and have to pay for the 'redundant' sections of the population through taxes and social charges. This kind of productivity development and growth increasingly destroys social integration, and erodes the living environment – both for those who have no work and for those who, because they are competing for better performance, lack the time and ability for varied human relations and leisure activities.

The enormous increase in labour productivity has not been matched by an equivalent development in efficiency in handling resources and productive factors. The exploitation of natural resources has grown enormously without the efficiency of their uses having risen comparably. Such a development not only disastrously undermines the foundations of future production and consumption, but also destroys the living environment of people – the basis of which is nature itself.

It is possible and necessary to embark on a new road of economic development, and to find a type of development which is in harmony with the environment and human needs. What is on the agenda is a socio-ecological transformation that can also be called a global revolution (Club of Rome) and must leave its mark on the 21st century. Three aspects of this transformation must be highlighted:

1. the transition to ecological sustainability, and the inevitable reorientation of production from manufacturing material goods to the production of real human wealth which is now possible – the universal needs, abilities, pleasures, productive forces, etc. of individuals produced in universal exchange (Karl Marx);

2. a global offensive for overcoming poverty, hunger and underdevelopment, and

3. a new era implementing the equality of sexes in politics, the economy, science, education, the media and culture. A modern Left does not, however, reduce the abolition of patriarchal power to a policy on equality. It regards the emancipatory struggles of women as one of the major movements for changes in society.

No less than a transformation of world society is on the agenda. An erosion of ruling structures touches on the predominance of capital utilisation over society, the destructive tendencies towards nature, the rule of the 'North' over the 'South', and the dominance of men over women.

The entire system of production services, housing, transport and way of life as existing in the 20th century must be converted. An efficient use of natural resources, and the ability to handle them 'productively', must improve in multiple ways in the next 20 years. These are the completely underdeveloped future markets requiring labour, capital and, most of all, knowledge. The ecological and social transformation will generate comprehensive innovation and investment processes and can lead to a net increase in jobs even in the mid-term.

In order to achieve this goal, a new framework for markets is indispensable. Amongst other things, it must include in prices the burdens resulting from economic activity for society which so far have not been included in business costs. Effective ecological taxes are needed to regulate economic activities and their social costs. Structural and regional policies can contribute to desirable developments. The new economy will be based on a globalised exchange of information, a far-reaching regionalisation of material and energy cycles, and localisation of many people-related services, enabling the regional labour capacity to be used to the full and environmentally-friendly economic cycles to be established. The necessary revolution leading to an efficient use of natural resources requires a reorientation of research and technology policy towards sustainable development.

Socio-ecological sustainability and a modernisation of the working society boil down to gainful employment and a reduction of the overall lifetime of work in differentiated and flexible forms for everyone. A modern working society must also make possible a new combination of gainful employment and creative communal and individual work. Finding versatile and meaningful fields for communal and individual work can start with the ecological transformation of private life. It must regain the power to shape communal affairs in local and regional areas, and will give rise to a host of social and cultural projects. Extending the opportunities for voluntary, communal and individual work forms the alternative to a continued subordination of social relations to the economy and commerce, as well as a further reduction of life to material consumption.

Creativeness and commitment must no longer be limited to individual careers in gainful employment, high incomes, and the exclusive consumption of the select few. Everyone should be employed – both with paying jobs and with personal work – according to their abilities and needs in order to find a sensible combination of work, life, enjoyment and personal fulfilment.

7. The growth of the low-wage sector results in a lasting division of society.
The alternative is to find new fields for sustainable development, and to reduce and diversify gainful employment as well as to increase its flexibility.
Growth oriented to the world market and reduction of wage costs will not solve the problem of mass unemployment. Traditional labour market policy is insufficient, and the creation of a low-wage sector polarises society and wrongly

subsidises businesses. Without establishing totally new fields for, and a redistribution of, gainful employment, society will suffer a lasting split between high income earners, their servants, and the unemployed.

The crisis in gainful employment can be resolved. A modern socialist policy must search for new ways which are closest to its goal – the free development of everyone. Three ways should be mentioned:

First, the future of work can be found in a transformation of production and production-related services, as well as the replacement of goods and technologies which pollute the environment by ecologically harmless ones. Second, since just 20 percent of those gainfully employed could provide the necessary material goods for society as a whole under today's level of productivity, we require a considerable extension of social, people-oriented services: education and training, health, upbringing, nursing care, scientific, cultural and sports activities, social and psychological care, counselling, support for self-help projects, social communication and environmental protection. These fields are inexhaustible for human activity. Already today the majority of people in the Western world are employed outside material production. Yet, the functioning of services should not be reduced to the provision of 'human capital' for businesses. People-oriented services form the core of the production of wealth in the 21st century. The current leisure industry is only the latest Fordist harbinger. The present-day Internet may be the early form of a new knowledge and communication society which still lies hidden in the folds of the old system, covered by commercials and passive entertainment.

Strategic decisions for a new path of development, for future-capable fields of employment, are indispensable. Yet, they must be twinned with institutional innovations. A modernised working society cannot limit itself to creating more jobs. It must give rise to institutions that are in line with the emergent social structures and circumstances of life. The modernisation processes of the past 50 years have eliminated the social conditions of a Fordist working world that were based on a male head of the family who was normally employed for a lifetime.

Nowadays, the biography of gainful employment is marked by various simultaneous and consecutive roles: yesterday a trainee, today self-employed and part-time worker, tomorrow unemployed, and the day after that maybe entrepreneur and, finally, a claimant receiving welfare. The diverse social roles can no longer be clearly attributed to certain social classes, strata and groups. That does not mean social injustice has decreased: on the contrary, it is growing. But there are no clear lines of classification left. There are workers, blue and white-collar, with rather high incomes, rich free-lancers, and also those who for many years live close to the poverty line, businesspeople who have gone broke without any social safeguard, rich and poor doctors, and some university graduates without a job or entitlement to social safeguards, and yet others with great material opportunities.

Consequently, the concentration on normal working relationships must be abolished, and the diversity of incomes and employment, and their combination, must be accounted for when setting up rules for gainful employment and laying out systems of social safeguards. The debate about pseudo-employment shows especially that the old categories have become anachronistic. Various forms of gainful employment, times of training and work in communal projects, or in an individual sphere must be combined flexibly and in the most diverse ways without people suffering a lack of income or social safeguards, and without the individual being able to wriggle out of their solidarity obligations towards the community.

The exploration of new ecological, social and cultural fields for gainful employment, and development of new forms thereof and their combination, are the fundamental condition for modernising work. At the same time, by shortening the average work-week for men and women to 30 hours, it should be possible to shorten the overall cycle of lifetime employment and thereby allow gainful employment to be combined with voluntary communal and individual work (unwaged).

Lifetime employment must be reduced in various and flexible forms. In this field a balance of interests between employee and employer is necessary and possible. Flexibility means various possibilities in terms of working hours. 'Working hour choice' could be a future possibility. It addresses more than just part-time work, training times, sabbatical and parental leave; and flexible replacement without facing social decline using the Northern European example. Offering working hour choice to older employees should provide them with an opportunity for making a smooth transition into retirement. People of 55 years and older should be legally entitled to old-age working hour choice. In terms of flexibility, thought should be given to an individual choice of working hours by the employees in the first place.

A large degree of non-profit jobs in the overall amount of work in society, and the specific features of many people-oriented services, simply cannot be subordinated to the yardstick of investment returns. Therefore, it is necessary to find out how these jobs can be classified.

In part they will have to be done as public work, as now, yet with more emphasis on citizens and their needs. At the same time, the non-profit sector or third sector should be jointly extended by private businesses and the state and organised by autonomous economic entities, instead of expanding the low-wage sector. Public institutions and organisations under local supervision could farm out new socio-cultural and ecological projects financed in part by public funding and partly by fees and prices. The businesses chosen to run the projects would have to live up to certain labour market, social, ecological and local political criteria. Through a structural policy and business philosophy, they should contribute to the emergence of relatively stable regional economic networks. This is where the third employment sector, receiving public funding, should come in. Another possibility would be the creation of individual income by combining social safeguards with an allowance for taking over socially meaningful jobs. Shorter working hours twinned with fundamental safeguards for times without employment should make it possible for the individual to find time for training in their own field of work, or for co-operation in non-profit or charitable projects of a cultural, ecological, social, scientific or pedagogical nature while in employment or instead of it.

8. Participation of citizens in the wealth of society does not, exclusively, mean more private consumption; rather, it will lead to a better quality of life for both women and men.

Abandoning a mode of consumption that reduces pleasure to consumerism and eventually leads to a worsening quality of life and stultification, does not mean forsaking the positive aspects of the Fordist consumer society. What is required is not the elimination of consumption, but the use of the material wealth, mobility, space and the world of goods in a different way. Consumption will bring pleasure and satisfaction if it reflects the variety of enjoyable behaviour and the richness of human relations. To this end the individual needs free time and work which he or she has chosen. This will not lead to a reduction of purchasing power and, ultimately, demand. Conversely, their increase must not be the only undifferentiated alternative to a one-sided policy on supply. Collective bargaining in the next century should also be used to translate rises in productivity into improvements in the quality of life. In one's own body, in bringing up the children, in private life, in the home and garden, in food and drink, in local affairs, in harmony with the environment and its preservation, there is no need for commercialisation, no expenses to be minimised, and no tasks that home servants or service-providers do. They form the private life, from which pleasure and satisfaction arise at least as much as from gainful employment and a career. The battles of the future will be more like battles about a new mode of living. A redistribution of opportunities in life is a fundamental condition for preserving cohesion in society, and democracy.

A tremendous reduction of the time spent working is an essential condition for women and men to be able equally to take part in gainful employment and work. That also opens up new opportunities for women's real involvement in the renewal of democracy. True equality requires that there are no obviously underpaid sectors which tie women, and also men, financially to their partners. A more co-operative working world, a new employment policy, and a more self-determined combination of gainful employment with voluntary work would make it possible for all to overcome the exploitation of stereotypical 'women's work' according to patriarchal socialisation (solidarity and readiness for caring, social sensitivity, willingness to compromise) in the mostly poorly paid service industries, and such behavioural orientation should have a much more central role.

In this and other fields the strength and development of trades unions is pivotal.

9. A new mode of development requires a change in economic regulation and institutional reforms, without which the new trend for a socially and ecologically transforming society cannot be moulded.

A social and ecological conversion means that a host of players – individuals, organisations, businesses, state authorities, etc. – must change their behaviour. Each far-reaching change of behaviour, therefore, requires a reform of institutions which regulate and structure behaviour. This is not done simply to juxtapose more regulation through either the market or the state. Institutions only work as well as they correspond with the opportunities and means of those involved. The regulatory system incorporating markets, big organisations, corporate bargaining procedures, detailed bureaucratic economic activity, exploitation of the environment, and a system of labour on the basis of an oligopoly under Fordism, is no longer in keeping with the social facts at the end of the 20th century. The traditional regulation of international markets and money in the world has collapsed without new and effective institutions having emerged.

Deregulation provides no solution. It is only a negative variation marked by a one-sided interest in dominating the market for the best interests of capital. A new path of development, therefore, requires institutional reforms especially in the fields of the economy, social and tax systems. When rearranging economic regulation the following currents, amongst other things, could be of importance:

Primarily, overall conditions must be set for the world markets establishing and enforcing comparable standards in the fields of political and social human rights, ecology, product quality and consumer protection. World markets need regulation that also guarantees opportunities for the economies of the less developed countries. Financial markets must be regulated in a fashion that does not hamper productive investment, but scales down speculation. Apart from agreements on environmental and social standards, a regulation of the international trade in capital seems to be most urgent. The introduction of (Tobin) taxes on foreign exchange and capital transfer, public supervision of banks, and less scope for the dollar and Euro are essential steps.

Without underestimating the difficulties of re-regulating world markets, far more initiative should be expected from the social democratic governments in Europe in this respect. The world market powers dominating in regions must take the lead. The fact that rich countries reject the introduction of certain environmental and social standards, citing international competition, is not only dishonest but also writes off the future.

The vast majority of institutions for an ecological regulation of the economy have yet to be established. The underlying principle would be that ecological resources, depending on their nature and importance, remain the property of the regional or local communities, nations or world population and cannot be privatised. Such resources can be used by private businesses in periods to be determined in exchange for compensation for the cost of reproduction of ecological resources, i.e. the cost of replacing or substituting rare ecological goods and the investment cost of long-term ecological conversion. Apart from eco-taxes achieving genuine ecological regulation, other suitable instruments could be certificates and environmental charges. They do not constitute any distortion of the economic balance. They simply correct the mistakes made because of insufficient inclusion of ecological costs in the calculations of businesses. Ecological conversion does not mean simply collecting the cost for using ecological resources. It also means using these revenues in a socially and ecologically meaningful way. First, it is necessary to ensure that those receiving very low pay are compensated for their additional burdens. Second, businesses must not be freed from ecological taxes by exceptional regulations, as the calculation of long-term ecological costs is urgently required. Wherever it is necessary and makes sense, the competitiveness of businesses is to be backed up by temporary capital aid, amongst other things, for investment to lower the consumption of resources and relieve the strain on natural cycles. Special support for small and medium-sized businesses should be done directly and not by way of cutting ecological taxes in defiance of the system in order to lower additional wage costs. Third, consumers must be able to compensate for the additional costs resulting from ecological taxation through environmentally friendly conduct. This calls for support for public and long-distance transport and energy conservation. This requires an ecological investment programme that re-invests the money coming from ecological taxes in efficiency-raising and economically meaningful projects. Businesses and authorities, through semi-public capital investment companies, could do this and create new jobs in the process.

Economic support could gradually be changed from subsidies which both perpetuate structures and distort competition to equity capital support for innovative investment. It should not come from the state. Democratic and public companies for economic support, based on equal representation, ought to organise it. In the long run economic support could, therefore, be shifted from the state budget to a considerable degree, and financed mainly from independent sources.

A number of public services obviously cannot be provided efficiently by state-owned companies in their current form. However, services for the common good are an obstacle to privatisation. Solutions that replace local state monopolies by supra-regional big companies in monopoly positions with no ties to either the region or local community are particularly problematic. That again requires a quest for new ways between state and private companies.

What is feasible is combinations of umbrella companies under public law and democratic supervision with the broadest possible participation. However, the state would not be in a management position. These companies would meet the needs of the customers through their services, together with a number of smaller and medium-sized companies. In this area pluralistic competition could be connected to public control. Such ideas must be followed up and tested. In this context it would make sense to introduce the legal form of a public company which the state appoints to run certain public services. It would act commercially, like any business in competition, and receive only temporary subsidies or none at all, and be under public supervision. Its profits would be used for the common good.

Eventually industrial relations and the system of co-determination must be revised. Big companies and their activities are not the capital owners' private business. Neither is it enough to incorporate only the interests of the workforce. It would be necessary to set up boards divided into thirds. Public interests, which the activities of the company touch on, could be represented by a public bank. These banks should not be represented by staff from state authorities, but by elected representatives of public non-governmental organisations.

10. A modernisation of the social system requires the participation of most people in financing it and introducing a demand-oriented social safeguard, ridding the solidarity-based insurance systems of out-of-area services, limiting entitlements and the obligation to pay for high income earners, more efficiency and democratic self-management in the use of funds, as well as universal standards for all mandatory insurance schemes.

The welfare state is a second field for institutional reform and regulation. Welfare and social systems developed and index-linked under Fordism such as health and pension insurance, unemployment and nursing-care insurance, have been subject to heated debates and insufficient attempts at reform for a long time. The reform of the health system and pension schemes which the German government has just ushered in holds a few correct approaches – especially the introduction of a fundamental safeguard – but has still more problems.

It is time for a reform of the social systems that complies with the social structures evolving in the 20th century, and supports the transition to a new ecological path of development, and a new connection between the economy and way of life. That mainly requires two big steps – a standardisation of social insurance and the introduction of a fundamental safeguard. In future, there should be only one mandatory basic and health insurance.

At a time of grave changes, and ever greater losses in social security, it is very urgent to introduce a new pillar in the systems of social security in exchange for other services, and fundamental social safeguards based on needs. The traditional reduction of social security to those in gainful employment must be abolished. A differentiation between services for civil servants, and separate insurance systems for blue and white collar workers, is untimely. There is a need for a social insurance system that insures all sections of the population against risks and provides basic safeguards in case they are necessary. In return, most forms of income should be used to fund it. Not only workers, but also entrepreneurs, free-lancers and self- employed people may need social security at some point. Above all, a pension system that takes full employment for a lifetime for granted to provide a normal pension is no longer in keeping with a society in which changing social roles and kinds of income are increasing in the course of a lifetime. Continuous security and stable premiums require that almost all kinds of income are used, and businesses pay in solidarity, however, on the basis of what is feasible economically.

Basic safeguards must guarantee conditions fit for human beings to live in. It is not enough to provide the material conditions for one's existence. This safeguard must not be misunderstood or abused as a 'gentle way to dispose of' people. It must open chances for actively taking part in social life, obtaining training and seeking a job as a worker or becoming self-employed, starting a business or a career.

A basic social safeguard must be available for everyone in need. The compulsory index-linked basic social safeguard does not need to cover completely the high living standard reached in life for those earning high incomes. They can see to that for themselves. The entitlement comes from premiums to be payable amounting to twice the basic social safeguard as a maximum, for example. Except for those unable to work, recipients of the safeguard (including pensioners) and children until the end of their education, everyone would have to pay a premium, depending on the kind of income. This would cover the funds necessary for meeting the payment commitments without raising rates. Earners of higher incomes pay into the solidarity-based insurance scheme up to a certain limit. Nothing has to be paid for the income exceeding that limit. However, they cannot claim any payments either for that part. Higher income earners can make their own provisions for beyond the income threshold. Apart from private insurance this can involve company pensions, collective social schemes, co-operative insurers and the like. Incomes from these sources are also free of premiums to the basic safeguards system. Welfare, unemployment benefit and allowance, and mandatory pensions could, in their present form, expire over a longer period. Procedures for granting them could be reduced to a minimum. Humiliating control procedures would be dropped because relatives' incomes, savings, etc. would be exempt. The mandatory basic safeguard would, therefore, replace today's pension and unemployment insurance schemes. As health and nursing-care insurance could also be standardised, there would be only two mandatory insurance schemes left to be paid for by income earners.

The contributory system is preferable to tax-financed systems (such as a basic state pension) because the latter can be changed arbitrarily according to a change of politics. The contributory system has a built-in quasi-ownership-based claim.

For children and young people up to age 18 an allowance covering all everyday costs would be paid as a basic safeguard. From age 18 they are entitled, when in need, to a minimum basic safeguard independently of their parents' income. This would also apply to students, replacing student loans.

Businesses must show solidarity and pay into the insurance funds. Payments would no longer be based on the gross wage costs. Net profits should form the basis. So far, businesses with relatively high labour costs relative to the overall costs, and more employees at comparable levels of turnover, have been disadvantaged. Now the changes would bring about a more just and functional division of costs.

It is possible immediately to rid the social security systems of out-of-area services and make, them more efficient in their use of social funds. Services for which no premium has been paid must be financed from taxes, if necessary by means of an insurance. A standardisation of the mandatory insurance schemes raises efficiency, eliminates unequal treatment, makes simpler laws possible, and scales down red tape. The insurance schemes' self-management must be extended and made more transparent.

11. The tax system must be fundamentally modernised, simplified, and made transparent, as well as oriented towards tax justice: lower taxes on small incomes, higher taxes on big private property and unproductively invested profits and revenues from financial investments. The public purse can be rehabilitated in a manner that paves the way to a more just social order and sustainable development.

A fundamental reform of the system of taxes and charges is urgently required. First of all, the Social Democrats' plan to broaden the basis for taxation by doing away with exceptions, subsidies and exemptions, and lowering the rate of taxation in return, is correct. The taxes businesses pay in Germany are not too high in absolute terms; the tax burden has been levied incorrectly and unjustly both from an economic and social standpoint between enterprises, the very wealthy and those dependent on wages.

The Social Democrats' approach does not suffice as a real reform of taxation legislation. It is an illusion that it is possible to lower incomes from enterprises and assets, taxes and charges for the middle classes, taxes for workers and the financially vulnerable, all at the same time, and yet gain enough scope for the state to manoeuvre in financial policy.

The crux of the problem is that German tax law no longer corresponds to the social facts at the end of the 20th century. An overdue modernisation must also introduce a reasonable differentiation between private households and businesses of unincorporated companies, so that the transfer of investments and profits between private households and enterprises can be taxed more justly. The separation between private households and enterprises must be adequately reflected in the arrangements of commercial, corporate taxation and social legislation. Re-invested profits and investments should be treated differently and taxed less than income transferred to private households. An increase in the value of a business, as long as it remains undistributed as part of the going concern, should be taxed less. In return, depreciation schemes for fictitious investment must be abolished because they only serve to avoid taxes on private incomes.

The variety of enterprises, on the one hand, and the different kinds of incomes, on the other, amongst the private households should be taxed in a comparable way. In particular, taxes on profits from, and transfers to, financial investments must be completely reorganised. The underlying principle should be here, too, that investments and reinvested profits are taxed less, and profits transferred to private households taxed more. Under this condition a wealth tax can be imposed, above all, on assets not invested for productive purposes. Profits used for, or stemming from, speculation must be taxed much more than profits resulting from production or services. The trend away from production towards speculation cannot be stopped otherwise. Only if profits from production are higher than those from speculation will there be a real chance to create jobs and contain and keep on a leash the dangerously uncontrolled international transfer of money.

Estate taxation could be arranged in such a way that assets remaining in a business are taxed less, while those transferred to private households above a certain threshold (which, for example, does not touch privately used housing property) are taxed more.

The public purse in Germany and in other leading Western nations has been slithering into a serious crisis for years, perceived mainly as a problem of public debt. Since the early 1980s, national debt has risen by 600 per cent in Germany; in 1997, the total amount of national debt exceeded more than 2,000 billion Deutschmarks. Almost one in four Deutschmarks of taxes now goes towards debt service. And the debts are growing. About 25 per cent of the 1999 budget is covered by loans and the sale of federal property.

As much as they are desirable, initial new trends in expenditure such as a continuous labour market policy, or the first steps towards the 100,000 roofs solar-collector programme, cannot be repeated next year without new solutions. The revenues from privatisation accrued this year can only be used once. These approaches have been reduced even more, and partly cancelled by the austerity programme. Weighty election promises, such as a rise in the housing allowance, the ecological transformation of society, and a modern innovation policy especially for small and medium-sized businesses, lack funds.

The crisis of public finances does not primarily arise from the fact that, so far, the road to social justice has been paved with ever higher levels of public spending, as Tony Blair and Gerhard Schroeder would have it. That does not go for the previous government in Germany. The crisis was mainly caused by the fact that the public purse lost that part of the revenues which used to come from corporate and wealth taxes. In fact, in Germany taxes on profits and incomes play an ever smaller part in overall tax revenues, while the share of wages taxes has risen by 20.7 per cent alone between 1992 and 1997, and constitutes the biggest item for the Treasury. The burden of taxes and charges on wages and salaries is much too high. Under the condition of Fordism in crisis, by and large, only the major corporations have received big tax breaks, for reasons of competition. Incomes from property rose more than proportionally. The consequent decrease in unemployment which was promised has failed to materialise. In fact, the number of unemployed clearly grew.

As to businesses, the myth of Germany as a high-tax country is not true: the actual average corporation tax is 21 per cent. According to the Organisation for Economic Co-operation and Development (OECD), amongst the industrialised nations only the Netherlands has a lower rate, while it is much higher in the United States (27 per cent), Denmark (28.6 per cent) and Great Britain (32.4 per cent). If German businesses were still taxed according to the 1980 regulations, the government would have 100 billion Deutschmarks more every year. The problem is that the major corporations avoid taxation, or are exempt from it, so that small and medium-sized enterprises as well as wage-earners must shoulder the main burden.

The crisis of the public finances must be resolved other than in the socially unjust way the German government is trying now. The following principles would have to apply:

Each Deutschmark earned above the poverty line (be it from wages, salaries, other earnings, profits and revenues) is subject to taxation with taxes rising progressively. Pensions, revenues from life insurance policies, and other old age incomes, as well as the basic social safeguard (as soon as it has been introduced), are exempt from taxation. In other words, the basis for taxation is broadened, exceptions are abolished, and effective instruments are applied to counter tax avoidance by big corporations, the rich, and loan and insurance companies. Higher taxes are levied on capital revenues from transactions in international financial and foreign exchange markets. More pressure is necessary to harmonise taxation legislation within the European Union.

The developments causing the crisis in public finances have beneficiaries and profiteers. Against the background of huge unsolved problems in society which require financing, and the unjust accumulation of wealth amongst the economically powerful, a temporary wealth charge on big property, and on the assets of insurance and loan corporations and investment companies, is necessary for a transitional period of ten years.

In the long run, fewer burdens with a decrease in mass unemployment and the reform of the welfare state, as well as revenues from embarking on new development roads, will pay off. A new kind of full employment would cut the costs of unemployment (about Deutschmark170 billion in Germany in 1998) tremendously, and clearly raise tax revenues.

All expenditures are being checked for their contribution to the necessary economic and socio-ecological conversion. Subsidy perpetuating structures are gradually being phased out. Support contributing to the socio-ecological transformation of society, and thus to a possible elimination of mass unemployment, are retained and extended.

The financial transfer to eastern Germany, and the competencies for decisions about that, are changed; a fund for social and ecological communal projects, or an innovation bank within the 'pilot project east', will be established.

By means of a reform of local finances, self-administration as decreed in the constitution will be established in a new way in local communities. They must be able positively to influence regional, ecologically oriented economic cycles, and to assume a leading part in establishing a third employment sector with public support.

12. International security and the preservation of peace mainly depend on a just world economic order, non-violent forms of implementing human rights and claims by ethnic, political and cultural groups, as well as a UN monopoly on the use of force.

From the experience of the most appalling of all wars in history, and the failure of the League of Nations, the United Nations Organisation and, in its Charter, an international law emerged which outlaws war, aims for consensus, and bases international relations on fundamental democratic principles. Furthermore, for nearly half a century the balance of terror prevented the terror of war in Europe.

The return of war to the European continent, its extension to Africa and Asia, its re-legitimisation by the policy pursued in the capitalist metropolises and countless other countries also results from the fact that the mutual fetters on the military arsenals in west and east were cut. Yet, most of all, it shows that there have never been real intentions to replace confrontational and military security concepts by co-operative and civilian ones. Gorbachev's New Thinking has turned out to be an ineffective episode for a civilian make-up of international relations. Readiness on the part of the west to let themselves in for such ideas was relinquished following the demise of the Warsaw Treaty and the Soviet Union.

International conflicts, the dangers of a variety of wars and proliferation of arms of mass destruction have increased. Unjust economic relations and underdevelopment, in which many countries of the South are still being kept, are causes of present-day crises and military disputes. These are accentuated by US and NATO ambitions to establish virtually a world-wide military monopoly on the use of force, the undemocratic nature of international relations, and disregard for human rights, international law and the rights of ethnic, political and cultural groups in many countries. Neo-liberal, radical globalisation jeopardises traditional social structures and alternative opportunities for development alike. It is flanked by cultural imperialism and the resistance it engenders. Without underestimating the specific causes in individual regions and countries, dictatorial regimes, ideological fundamentalism, wars about distribution, and a world-wide militarisation of politics are largely the consequence of economic, political and military strategic decisions by the metropolis countries.

Currently, anti-militarist forces are weak, and the monopoly of the west on the use of force is hardly restricted. However, building politics on that assumption is short-sighted, counter-productive and irresponsible. It creates new tensions and aggravates old ones, destroys civilised and co-operative thinking and, at best, solves warring conflicts by causing new and, in the long run, probably worse ones. Universal applicability of human rights, and individual freedom and democracy cannot be brought about by military threats or war, and are not really intended. But the granting of human rights is a requirement for lasting peace.

Those who want to pursue a policy based on finding means to prevent new wars, and to remove and contain existing military conflicts, must reduce the instruments of war, and primarily the dominating military power of NATO. First, disarmament must again be in the focus of international politics: arms exports must be downsized and eventually banned altogether. The manufacture of new arms and especially high tech weapons, and the extension of the attack-capable armed forces, must be effectively limited or stopped. The proliferation of weapons of mass destruction can only be prevented by disarmament on the part of the nuclear powers themselves.

Second, new legal curbs on war as a political instrument are required: such a policy must be halted, and the UN monopoly on the use of force rehabilitated. Surrendering sovereignty in terms of security policy to democratised international institutions could provide joint security with a reliable basis. Not the enlargement of NATO and the extension of its military strategy, or an activation of the Western European Union as the military wing of the European Union, but a decisive strengthening and democratisation of the United Nations and the Organisation for Security and Co-operation in Europe (OSCE) offers a way out of the spiral of wars.

Thirdly, a just world economic order and the opening of alternative and freely determined chances for development for the countries of the South is the most important prerequisite for removing the causes of dangerous regional battles over distribution, and regional ambitions for supremacy and local militarism.

Fourth, civilian crisis prevention, an international crisis early warning system, and peace education and research must assume a totally new status. Non-violent and effective forms of implementing human rights, as well as the rights of ethnic, political and cultural groups, could complement existing instruments under international law.

Peace, too, can only result from politics. The consequences of the current world economic policy, present strategies in security policy, the traditional instrumentalised human rights for power politics, and current western attitude towards the UN and OSCE are unsuited to peace. The socialist Left must contribute to a new beginning in each of these fields.

The Third Way off the Rails

Philip Bagwell

Philip Bagwell is the author of The Transport Crisis in Britain *(Spokesman Books, £9.99).*

Following the rail disaster at Ladbroke Grove near Paddington at 8.11am on 5 October 1999, the London *Evening Standard* of that date reported that

> 'investigators will be concentrating their efforts on whether a signal was passed at danger or whether there was some sort of signalling or track fault which allowed the trains to collide.'

The *Guardian* reporter two days later was more precise. He wrote in the first paragraph of the front page:

> 'the cause of Britain's worst rail disaster in 50 years was confirmed as the driver of one of the trains passing a red signal.'

In fact, seven other drivers had passed through at red the notorious Signal 109 at Ladbroke Grove, which Railtrack had failed to re-site, as recommended by the traindrivers' union ASLEF. The Health and Safety Executive (HSE) had pointed out that there were 22 other sites in the United Kingdom which had been passed through at red more than five times.

However, the first interim report of the Health and Safety Executive on 8 October gave a significantly different interpretation of events at Ladbroke Grove. It stated:

> 'Our belief is that it is a systems failure and that any action or omission on the part of the driver is a systems failure and that any action or omission on the part of the driver was only one factor.'

So what was this systems failure? It would be easy to pick on particular shortcomings in the operation of railways in late 1999 – old and new rolling stock simultaneously in use; ultra-modern signal boxes manned with signalmen struggling with antiquated ones further down the line, rundown stations and extravagantly spruced up ones, and so on. But it is essential to recall at least the events of the '80s and '90s in order to understand why the collision of the morning of the 5th October was 'an accident waiting to happen'.

During the ministry of Margaret Thatcher from 1979-1990, in transport policy the emphasis was given to building motorways with the object of creating a 'car owning democracy'. Since it was the accepted government philosophy that high government spending on state-owned industries 'crowded out enterprise', public service obligation (PSO) grants, brought in by Barbara Castle in her Transport Act of 1968, were drastically reduced (as shown in Figure 1). The reduction of both the PSO and the External Financing Limit (EFL) (on the amounts that British Rail (BR) was allowed to borrow), meant that BR was obliged to restrict itself to essential maintenance and renewal. The industry was starved of government financial support when compared with other European countries, as is shown in Figure 2. Despite this deprivation, in the Major government's White Paper *New Opportunities for the Railways: the Privatisation of British Rail* published in July 1992, it was admitted that

> 'the efficiency of British Rail compared well with that of other European railways. The productivity of the BR workforce is among the highest of any European railway.'

This assessment was confirmed in British Rail's *Annual Report and Accounts for 1994-95*, which revealed that, in the year to 31 March 1994, the train kilometres run (loaded and empty) per member of staff employed was 3,363, compared with an average of 2,200 of the 14 other member states of the Community of European Railways (CER).

Figure 1
Passenger Grants from Central Government (Public Service Obligation)
£m at 1988-89 prices

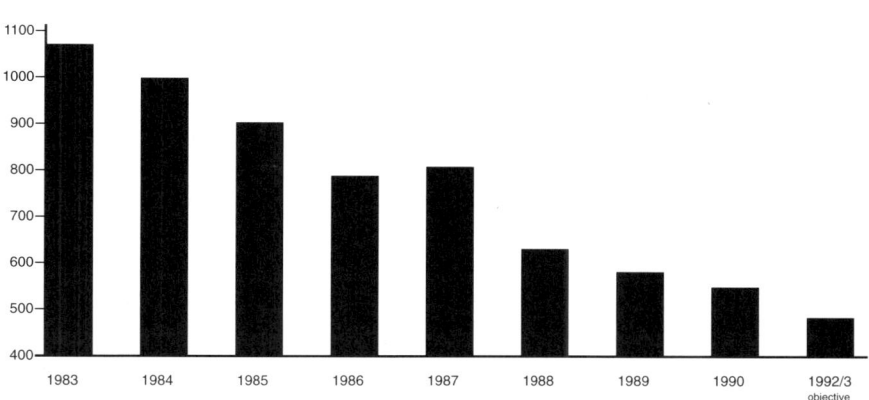

Sources: BRB Annual Report and Accounts, 1983. BRB Corporate Plan, 1988.

The External Financing Limit (EFL) was reduced from £1,100 million in 1983 to under £400 million in 1988-9 (both at 1988-9 prices). The result of these drastic restraints on BR's external financing was that Britain's railways have the lowest level of support per train kilometre of the 10 railway systems shown in Figure 2.

After John Major succeeded Margaret Thatcher as Prime Minister, the parliamentary pressure of those described by the late Robert Adley MP (Conservative) as 'anti-nationalisation fanatics' continued at an even more strident tempo. Although Margaret Thatcher had hesitated about privatisation as a root and branch policy for railways, the more strident right-wing element in the party had no hesitation. When the Conservatives were re-elected under John Major in 1992 the intended legislation was spelt out in the White Paper *New Opportunities for the Railways*, published in July 1992. According to Philip Stevens, the Railways Bill of 1993 was 'shaped in the cause of narrow political advantage, rather than that of an efficient and safe railway system'.[1] Although John Major's approval rating was over 50 per cent at the time of the General Election of 9 April 1992, and his party enjoyed a clear majority of 21 members over all other parties, his party's popularity fell like a stone in the following months, through evidence of sleaze among its leading members and through Norman Lamont (Chancellor of the Exchequer) falling out with his leader on the management of the economy. From May 1993 to May 1997 the Government sustained 10 bye-election defeats. At Christchurch on 29 July 1993 the Liberal Democrat vote rose to 65.1 per cent from the general election figure of 37.2 per cent, and at Staffordshire South-East the Labour Party's vote rose from 38.2 to 60.1. In June 1994 Major's approval rating fell to a mere 18 per cent.[2]

The next general election date was looming ever nearer. It would have to be not later than May 1997. Urgent action had to be taken to persuade the electorate

Figure 2
Government Subsidies in £s per Train Kilometre, 1986

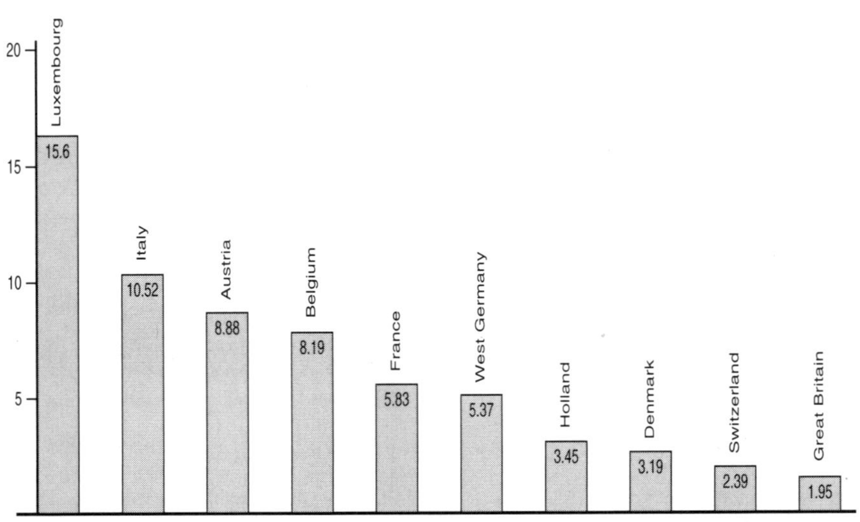

Sources: BRB Annual Report and Accounts, 1986. *The Observer*, 2nd July 1989.

to return to the Tory fold. Revenue from the sale of companies under the provisions of the Railways Act, 1993 was needed to finance vote winning (it was assumed) tax reductions. By the mid nineties 'revenue from sales had become an integral part of the budget arithmetic'.[3]

The Railways Bill was introduced into the House of Commons on 2 February 1993. The Government's plans to establish a separate company – Railtrack – to own and manage the track, stations and signals, alongside 25 railway operating companies to run the passenger train services and rolling stock leasing companies met with a storm of opposition. Nicholas Ridley, who was Margaret Thatcher's Secretary of State for Transport from 16 October 1983 to 21 May 1986, wrote an article in *The Times* in October 1992, headed 'Simply no way to run a railway', arguing that the separation of Railtrack from the franchise operators was 'a recipe for confusion'. Despite these expressions of concern, party loyalty prevailed. The second reading was carried on 27 February 1993 by 303 votes to 269. The doubters and hesitant hoped to carry amendments at the committee stage. They fought hard to effect changes and it took no less than 35 sessions to consider the 250 amendments tabled by both Government and Opposition. John MacGregor, the then Transport Secretary, made some concessions, such as making it a requirement that the Department of Transport should publish an investment plan in its annual report, but he refused to allow BR to bid in competition with private companies and individuals to be allocated operating franchises. It was on this issue that the House of Lords crossed swords with the government when the Bill came before it on 5 July. All those former Secretaries of State for Transport who had been made life peers, opposed it. Lord Peyton, who had served as Minister for Transport Industries in the Heath Government moved the key amendment to clause 22 of the Bill:

'Nothing in subsection (1) above shall prevent (a) the British Railways Board . . . or (b) a wholly owned subsidiary of the Board from having a franchise.'

He said:

'The amendment would let British Rail in. In effect it would be a step back from the clear intention of the Bill to kill off BR and bury the corpse at an early date.'[4]

Baroness Castle said that until then:

'nobody had suggested that the public should be excluded from showing whether it could compete on merit. It was a total tyranny to brand BR as a failure, as the noble lord (The Earl of Caithness) had done. He does not wish it to be allowed to prove whether it can compete.'[5]

Lord Peyton was successful in carrying this most important of the hundreds of amendments to the Bill proposed in the Upper House. Enough Tory, Liberal and cross bench peers supported the Labour group to carry the day by 150 votes to 112. Through the cessation of business in the summer recess it was not until 1 November that the Commons considered the Lords' amendments. With severely limited time for debate because the government passed a guillotine motion, the Commons rejected the Lords' proposed amendment on 2 November. On the following evening, meeting in the knowledge that the Bill would have to pass both Houses by the following morning, 4 November, the close of the session, if it was to survive, the Lords surrendered to the Commons at 11.30pm on Wednesday 3 November. The Bill received the Queen's signature on 5 November and came into operation on 1 April 1994. On this occasion those peers who resisted the Major government's frenzied efforts to push their privatisation Bill through parliament were acting in accordance with the views of railway users. A Gallop poll conducted on behalf of the *Daily Telegraph* in May 1993 revealed that 71 per cent of them were against the Government's plans. An even larger percentage – 84 per cent – were in favour of increasing British Rail's investment in the industry.

Once the Railways Bill had become law the Major Government's problem was to persuade members of the industry and the members of the investing public to put their money into the newly created private rail undertakings. The most important new company was Railtrack because of its ownership of the track, signals and the stations. A substantial downgrading of its assets was thought to be necessary in view of the threat of a possible incoming Labour government carrying out its promise of greater public control of the railways. However, the other side of the coin was that the Major Government's undervaluation of the railway's assets, combined with the complete absence of any safeguards against their subsequent resale at greatly enhanced prices, gave the green light to investors who were more interested in making a quick fortune instead of working for the improvement in the safety and efficiency of railway operations.

The two major examples of companies who took advantage of this loophole were Railtrack and three rolling stock leasing companies.

In the last Annual Report and Accounts of the British Railways Board – that for 1994-95 – the Board's auditors stated that the gross value of 'buildings and infrastructure (i.e. stations, signal boxes, offices and track) was £6,464 million as at 1 April 1994.[6] But at the sale on 20 May 1996 Railtrack's assets were given as £1.9 billion, an exceptionally good bargain which would guarantee a return of anything from 13 to 20 per cent in the first financial year. The enormity of this downgrading of an essential public asset can be seen by the fact that all the track, stations and signals of the UK were sold off for less than it cost to build London's Jubilee Line extension. Railtrack's real character as an organisation was revealed on the occasion of its flotation on the stockmarket, in May 1996, when the company's prospectus emphasised its marketable assets in land. There were thousands of acres of unused land by stations, former goods and marshalling lands, etc., which when developed could yield substantial profits. In the Commons on 17 April, 1996, David Chidgery cited one 'share shop' whose brochure stated:

'Railtrack is essentially a property company and the land that Railtrack will own could be regarded as one of the most valuable pieces of real estate in the United Kingdom.'[7]

The subsequent history of Railtrack reveals that its prime interest has been developing its most profitable assets as commercial centres. Travellers passing through Euston station concourse in recent years have noted the substantial increase in the area leased to shops. A few weeks before the Paddington rail disaster a splendidly, and expensively, redesigned Paddington Main Line Station was opened. In the company's Annual Report and Accounts, for 1998-9 (p.5), the Chairman boasted that

'The results of the £1 billion station refurbishments are everywhere to be seen.'

The sale by Railtrack of disused rail lines continued in 1999 to be an important source of income to the company despite the government having banned it in August 1998.[8] Back in April 1994 when it took over responsibility for the track, signalling and stations from BR, it announced that 'it planned to make substantial cuts in maintenance and repair bills'.[9] One feature of its policy of 'substantial cuts' was the policy of reducing rail replacement from 2.5 per cent of the track annually – as was the practice of BR and is the practice in Europe – to 1.5 per cent. One consequence of this cheeseparing was a sharp increase in the number of rail breaks. The Health and Safety Executive in August 1999 reported that the number of broken rails on the national rail network had risen by 21 per cent in the previous 12 months, while Vic Coleman, the chief inspector of railways, described the increased number of cases – up from 801 to 973 – as 'a major worry'.[10]

The change in railway practice and culture was highlighted by a shareholder of Railtrack who analysed the pages of the six-monthly report *Railtalk* he had just received. He wrote:

'The management culture of the railways has shifted perceptibly towards explicit bonus-linked goals of train performance and away from an absolute safety requirement.'[11]

In March 1994 BR established three companies as wholly owned subsidiaries. These became known as ROSCOs (rolling stock companies) which had ownership of 11,258 vehicles (carriages and locomotives, but not Eurostar or freight waggons). On 12 August the ownership of the three leasing companies was transferred from BR to the Secretary of State for Transport for a sum of £745 million, paid to BR. The Department of Transport decided that because the three companies would be operating in a competitive market, TOCs (Train operating companies) could choose from which company they could lease their rolling stock, there was no need for them to be subject to the jurisdiction of the Railway Regulator.[12] The sale by BR to three rolling stock companies was hurried as the Major Government had planned the launch of Railtrack in May 1996, some of the TOCs had yet to receive bidders and investors needed to be persuaded that there were opportunities for making easy money quickly. Table 1 summarises how what

Table 1

Company	Price paid to BR in November 1995	Price paid on resale and date	Profit from resale	Percentage gains to ROSCOs
Porterbrook	£527 million	£826 million August 1996	£298 million	56%
Angel	£580 million	£1.1 billion December 1997	£520 million	58%
Eversholt	£518 million	£726.5 million February 1997	£206.2 million	40%

the National Audit Office described as 'very substantial gains', were achieved.[13]

What was not reported in the National Audit Office Report was the fortunes made by management in the resale of the assets of the three companies. Sandy Anderson, Porterbrook's managing director, reportedly pocketed £33.8 million when the sale to Stagecoach was signed, the Eversholt team made a profit of £57.2 million on a stake of just £400,000, while Nomura of Angel netted £330 million.[14] The total profits from the resale made by the three management teams exceeded £1 billion, a sum which could have made a substantial improvement to the safety system on the railway network.

The obsession with cutting costs (including making railway workers redundant) affected the 25 TOCs as well as Railtrack and the ROSCOs. Between 1 April 1993 and 31 March 1994, the last year of public ownership, a Passenger Service Obligation (PSO) grant of £930 million was disbursed for the support of the social railway. In the following year, the first under privatisation, the Office of Passenger Rail Financing (OPRAF) took over PSO business from BR and the government allowed it to spend £1,717.8 million. (In round terms – since there were incidental expenses incurred in the transfer – doubling of allowances from one billion to two billion pounds.) In view of public protests about the size of the hand-outs to the TOCs it was provided that these hand-outs would be reduced to £1.2 billion by the year 2000. The prospect of having to make do with a reduced level of public support sharpened the call for an economy drive.[15] Although some regional companies managed to provide a good service, and their ability to do so was constrained by the failure of Railtrack to provide adequate improvements in the tracks and signalling, there were outstanding cases of failure to provide an adequate service. In an ill-considered effort of cost cutting early in 1997 South West Trains made 200 of its drivers redundant, only to find shortly afterwards that it had to cancel a number of its trains because it lacked drivers to run them. The nationwide reaction of the members of ASLEF can well be imagined. It is not difficult to understand the problem the TOCs had in finding trainee drivers. Driver Michael Hodder of the Thames train that collided with the First Great Western express (and paid for the collision with his life), had only seven months training and two months experience of driving on the very congested rails out of Paddington.[16]

Rail users have become more and more dissatisfied with the conditions of rail travel. The Central Rail Users Consultative Committee Report (CRUCC – the travellers watchdog) for 1998-99 dealt with a record 18,771 complaints over the year, 27 per cent more than had been made in the previous year.[17] Most of the complaints were about train delays of which 33.7% were due to faults in the infrastructure or in signalling, the responsibility of Railtrack.[18] Of the eight regional committees of the CRUCC the greatest number of complaints was received by the Western Region which First Great Western Railway dominates.[19] Nationally, complaints about punctuality increased in the year by 38% to 4,014; those on reliability and cancellations by 47% to 1,705 and overcrowding by 36% to 980.[20] These figures are a disgrace to a modern railway.

The splitting up of BR into 25 operating companies, Railtrack, the ROSCOs, manufacturing – a total of over 100 – has produced a vast bureaucracy, with consequent delays and misunderstandings. It is ironical that in moving the Second Reading of the Railways Bill, John MacGregor claimed that BR:

> 'combined the classic shortcomings of the traditional nationalised industry. It is an entrenched monopoly. That means too little responsiveness to customer needs . . . Inevitably also it has the culture of a nationalised industry, a heavily bureaucratised structure . . . an instinctive tendency to ask for more taxpayers' subsidy.'[21]

The actual outcome of the passing of the Railways Act was the creation of an 'entrenched monopoly' over stations, track and signals by Railtrack, the asking for more taxpayers' subsidy to double the amount given in the time of BR, and the heavily bureaucratised structure which was the inevitable consequence of the creation of 100 new companies.

As far back as March 1998 the House of Commons Environment Transport and Regional Affairs Committee suggested that Railtrack should be stripped of its power to oversee its own safety standards.[22] Within days of the Paddington crash, John Prescott announced that, because of its failure to carry out improvements in signalling and track renewal on the scale that the Health and Safety Executive deemed vitally necessary, he would take that responsibility away from Railtrack. But this action alone is no solution to the crisis on the railways. In any case Gerald Corbett, its chief executive, might be only too pleased to be rid of the most worrying and unrewarding part of his business so that he could concentrate on the profitable activity of converting large parts of station termini into shopping centres.

The railways should be restored to public ownership for both practical and moral reasons. With fragmented ownership there are more opportunities for individual companies to evade responsibility. For example, when two or more companies share the use of part of the railway network, or when a passenger has to change trains and a connection is missed, it is easy enough for the person at the enquiry desk to say, 'I'm sorry, Sir/Madam, but the other company's train did not wait for ours to arrive'. With one public owned body responsible for providing rail services the rolling stock needs of the whole system can be assessed and better terms obtained from the railway carriage and waggon manufacturing side of the business through placing bulk orders.

A great deal of modernisation and investment is required within the system. A big example of this is the need for more to be spent on electrification. In the UK less than one-third of the rail network has been electrified. This is considerably less than is the case of France, Belgium, the Netherlands, Italy and Spain.[23] Electrification is needed for train reliability, passenger comfort and safety. The reason why over 30 persons were killed and dozens more travellers received severe burns from the accident on 5 October 1999 was that the diesel fuel tanks under the carriages of one of the trains were fractured and their contents burst into flames. With electric traction there would have been no conflagration and it is likely that the number killed would have been less than 10. An overall plan is needed for more electrification of the rail network of the UK.

Under privatisation the financial return for investors is given greater priority than service and safe travel for passengers. Louise Christian, the chief counsel for the prosecution in the 1997 Southall rail crash enquiry, informed the public on 6 October 1999, the day after the Paddington disaster, that:

> 'A memorandum to the board of Railtrack on February 1995 warned that the cost of installing Automatic Train Protection (ATP) would affect the share value on its flotation.'[24]

She headed her article 'They kill to save money' – a stark and personalised heading, no doubt, but one expressing her conclusions after months of studying the facts of rail disasters and the feelings of the bereaved.

The UK desperately needs a rail system based on entirely different principles from those that currently govern the industry. The priority should be to provide a public service run as efficiently as modern technology, and sound business administration will allow, but with the welfare of passengers and staff the uppermost consideration.

In 1897 Clement Edwards, a Liberal MP and barrister of the Middle Temple, wrote that:

> 'The wastes of the present system, with its manifold ownership and multiplied managements, are enormous.'[25]

Ninety eight years later three Labour MPs, Michael Meacher, Henry McLeish and Glenda Jackson wrote a pamphlet *Runaway Train* and estimated the costs, thus far, of the transition to private ownership to be £1,250 million. They favoured a return to public ownership.

There are plenty of examples of efficiently run publicly owned railways within the 15 countries of the European Union. The European Commission has endeavoured to persuade them to introduce more competition in railway operation, particularly by separating the infrastructure from railway operation. In response France separated the two but retained public ownership of both functions by creating two publicly owned corporations. Sweden opened rail operations to competing company bids but allowed SJ, the state owned railway company, to bid with the consequence that it won over 90 per cent of the railway services.

Between 1985 and 1991 there were three serious accidents associated with signals, and costing the loss of 96 lives, on the state owned SNCF in France. In 1991, following the last disaster Jon Henley in Paris wrote 'For the French public it was one signalling accident too many'. Millions of francs were then spent on making the signalling systems safe. There were no serious accidents after this capital expenditure. SNCF spends at least four times as much public money on its railways as does the UK. It is realised that a reliable, fast and safe railway system will attract people from their cars or even, in the case of the Paris-Lyon route, from air travel.

The cost of returning railways to public ownership in the UK should be balanced against the high cost of congestion and accidents on the roads, estimated by the CBI as long ago as 1987 to be as high as £15 billion.

The return to public ownership (in a more democratically organised form than that of BR) should be financed by long term Treasury bonds at 4.5%-5%, a substantially cheaper way than by Public Private Partnership which can cost up to 12%, as the experience of financing Eurotunnel, and the approaches to it, certainly shows. It is said that the Treasury currently has a nest egg of some £8 billion. Some of this money should be invested *in a productive way* in improving the UK's railways. Parliament should abolish the Public Sector Borrowing Requirement limit to make this possible.

Footnotes

1. *Financial Times*, 8 October 1999.
2. David Butler and Gareth Butler, *British Political Facts 1900-94*, pp.258-9, pp.292-4.
3. *Independent*, 30 November 1994.
4. Lords, Hansard, Vol.547 No.164, 5 July 1993 cols. 1069-70.
5. *Ibid.*, cols 1081-2.
6. British Railways Board, Annual Report and Accounts, 1994-5, p.59. On 1 January 1994 the *Financial Times* estimated Railtrack's replacement cost as £7 billion.
7. House of Commons, Hansard, Vol.275, 17 April 1996 col. 748.
8. Statement by the Rail Freight group reported in the *Financial Times*, 27 April 1999. Railtrack Annual Report and Accounts Chief Executive's Report, 1998-9.
9. *Public Enterprise*, The Journal of the Public Enterprise group, No.44, September 1996 article on 'The Cost of Privatisation', pp.1-3.
10. *Railnews*, September 1999, p.5.
11. *Financial Times*, 10 October 1999.
12. National Audit Office, *Privatisation of the rolling stock leasing companies*, 5 March 1998, p.11, section 1.6.
13. NAO Report p.47 section 2 p.1.
14. *Financial Times*, 2 August 1996.
15. *The Guardian*, 23 December 1996.
16. *The Times*, 13 October 1999.
17. CRUCC *Report* 1998-99, p.13.
18. *Ibid.*, p.29.
19. *Ibid.*, p.31.
20 *Ibid.*, p.33.
21. Commons, Hansard, 6th Ser. Vol.222, 30 March 1993, col. 156.

22. *Guardian*, report, 15 March 1998.
23. HMSO *Transport Statistics Great Britain*: Section International Comparisons: Road and Rail Infrastructures (1996), p.166.
24. *Guardian*, 6 October 1999.
25. Clement Edwards *Railway Nationalisation* (1897), Second Edition revised 1907, p.20.
26. J. Henley, 'French blame neglectful British', *Observer* 10 October 1999.

This discussion of the Third Way will continue in the next issue of *The Spokesman*, including Frithjof Schmidt and Frieder Otto Wolf on 'The Green response to the Third Way: core values and framework policy statement and political prospects after a year of red-green government' in Germany.

THE BERTRAND RUSSELL PEACE FOUNDATION

THE LONDON BULLETIN

1999   Number 73

EUROPEAN CONFERENCE ON PEACE AND HUMAN RIGHTS

The Bertrand Russell Peace Foundation has been consulting widely about the new tensions that have been generated as a result of the recent war against Yugoslavia. Everywhere peace movements were divided during the war, as was wider European society. But, whatever positions were taken up during the conflict, we all now find ourselves in a qualitatively new position.

NATO has established a base in the Balkans, albeit slightly qualified by its more fraught relationship with the United Nations and the Government of Russia. But all the signs are that Kosovo will remain occupied for a long time, and that further conflicts may erupt in the region.

Outside the region, severe economic and political difficulties grip Russia, Ukraine and Belorus. Military confrontations trouble the Caucasus. Recently, Secretary Cohen went to Georgia and presented Mr Shevardnadze with a flight of helicopters 'to police the frontier'. Chechnya is again engulfed in war.

How can we restore and improve the capacity to resolve international confrontations without recourse to war? How can we create the necessary instruments to protect human rights where they are abused? Do we have an adequate framework within which to organise international solidarity actions? Would it be useful to organise a European Conference on Peace and Human Rights? If so, upon what crucial questions should its programme be founded?

The times have changed a great deal since we launched the so-called 'Russell Appeal' for European Nuclear Disarmament. We have not yet won that disarmament, although we are told that the cold war is over. Our agenda today includes a lot of unfinished business, and faces new dangers which we never imagined possible in the worst days of the cold war.

Amongst those who have so far endorsed the Appeal for this conference are members of different political parties and groups, including three Green MEPs and a number of members of the Confederal Left Group in the European Parliament. An important step forward was made at the meeting of the Confederal Left Group in Helsinki on the 21st October 1999, which Ken Coates of the Russell Foundation addressed. It was agreed then that it would be useful to explore further the possibility of convening a Conference on Peace and Human Rights, drawing together political groupings, NGOs and peace movements, and relevant organisations concerned with human rights from both West and East Europe.

A preliminary list of those who have already endorsed the proposal for a Conference follows:

Alavanos Alexandros MEP
Tariq Ali, New Left Review
Mike Allen, Dublin
Elmar Altvater, Berlin
Odd Andreassen, trade unionist, Norway
John Arden, playwright, Galway, Ireland
Jaime Ballesteros, OSPAAAL, Madrid
Rezso Banyasz, Hungarian Neutrality Foundation, Budapest
Michael Barratt Brown, economist
Brian Bastin, Salisbury
Tony Benn MP
Irene Brennan, peace activist, London
Mary Brennan, Christian CND
Howard Cheney, peace movement activist
Noam Chomsky, writer, USA
Andrew Coates, Labour Party, Ipswich
Roger Cole, Chair, Peace & Neutrality Alliance, Co. Dublin, Ireland
Rev'd Brian Cooper, World Disarmament Campaign, Edinburgh, &
    international Christian Peace Conference
Colin Crouch, Labour Party, London
Francoise Diehlmann, International Appeal of 15th May
Ernest Dyer, Labour Party, Kent
Pierre Galand, President, European Forum for North-South Solidarity, Brussels
Per Gahrton MEP
A Geranios, Physics Dept., University of Athens
Chris Gifford, Labour Party, Wales
Peter Gowan, New Left Review
Alasdair Gray, Glasgow
Joseph Halbersztadt, Warsaw
C H Hermanson, Stockholm, Sweden
Inna Ilivitzvey, Helsinki, Finland
Carl G Jacobsen, Carleton University, Canada
Jimmy Jancovich, France
Inger V Johansen, Red-Green Alliance, Copenhagen
Monty Johnstone, Green Socialist Network, London
Sylvia-Yvonne Kaufmann MEP
Bruce Kent, Hague Appeal
Ulla Klotzer, Finland
Andros Kyprianou, Head of International Relations, AKEL, Cyprus
Jean Lambert MEP
Peter Lanyon, Suffolk

Tom Leonard, Glasgow
Caroline Lucas MEP
Henry McCubbin, former MEP, Ayr
Steve McGiffen, Spectre Magazine
Frank McManus, Todmorden
John Maguire, peace activist, Cork, Ireland
Alice Mahon MP
Lucio Manisco MEP
Pedro Marset Campos MEP
Zhores Medvedev, scientist and writer
Adrian Mitchell, poet, London
Bjoern Moeller, Secretary General, International Peace Research Association,
    (CIPRAS), Denmark
Luisa Morgantini MEP
David Morris, Chairman, CND Wales
Jim Mortimer, former General Secretary, Labour Party
Wolf-Dieter Narr, Freie Univ. Berlin, Germany
Stan Newens, Labour Party
Milos Nikolic
David Norris, Slavonic Studies, Nottingham University
Jan Oberg, Transnational Foundation for Peace & Future Research, Lund, Sweden
Christine Oddy, former MEP, Coventry
Mikis Peristerakis, Peace Movement, Athens
Carsten Vesteragen Petersen, International. Secretary, Socialist Peoples Party,
    Denmark
Harold Pinter, Playwright
Tom Pitstra, GroeenLinks, Utrecht, Holland
Malcolm Pitt, Catholic World of Work Committee
Chris Purnell, Orpington Labour Party Kent
Jimmy Reid, journalist, Glasgow
Sergio Ribeiro
Professor Roland Roth, Berlin
Michael Rustin, Co-Editor, Soundings magazine
Richard Seebohm, Quaker Council for European Affairs, Brussels
Rev'd Norman Shanks, Iona Community, Scotland
Rae Street, Vice-Chair, CND
Ben Thompson, peace activist, Suffolk
Dorothy Thompson, Worcester
Kate Thompson, peace activist, Co. Galway, Ireland
Gyula Thurmer, President, Hungarian Workers' Party, Budapest
Antonia Tomassini, Italy
Tony Topham, Historian
Panos Trigazis, International Secretary, Synaspismos, Athens
David Turner, Edinburgh

Luigi Vinci MEP
Kurt Vonnegut, writer, USA
Harry Warner, peace activist, Manchester
Alan Whitford, FURI Bulletin, London
Jenny Williams, London
Eva Zetterberg, Stockholm, Sweden

CND CONFERENCE

Tony Simpson and Ken Fleet represented the Russell Foundation at this year's conference, which met in London in September. The conference heard a stunning presentation on current nuclear weapons development in the United States by Jacqueline Cabasso *of the Western States Legal Foundation in Oakland, California. She is a founding member of the Abolition 2000 Global Network to Eliminate Nuclear Weapons. These extracts are taken from her paper* Nuclear Hypocrisy: New Weapons Development and Anti-Disarmament Policies in the US, *dated February, 1999. The full text is available from the Foundation at 1440 Broadway, Suite 500, Oakland, CA 94612, USA.*

'. . . Contrary to its public pronouncements, the US is modernising and upgrading its nuclear forces and renewing its commitment to reliance on nuclear weapons, a reality which threatens the long-term viability of both the Nuclear Non-Proliferation Treaty (NPT) and the Comprehensive Test Ban (CTB).

'Presidential Decision Directive 60 (PDD), signed in December 1997, reaffirms the fundmental elements of US nuclear doctrine since World War II. According to newspaper accounts, the PDD re-commits the US to policies of threatened first use and threatened massive retaliation, and affirms that the US will continue to rely on nuclear arms as a cornerstone of its national security for the "indefinite future". In addition, the PDD reportedly contemplates nuclear retaliation against the use of chemical and biological arms – a policy called "counterproliferation".

'The PDD is backed by a major new programme to upgrade the US weapons infrastructure. The so-called "Stockpile Stewardship" programme is intended to retain "all historical capabilities of the weapons laboratories, industrial plants and the Nevada Test Site", without underground testing. Stockpile Stewardship will provide design capabilities potentially greater than those available during the Cold War. It encompasses a test site ready to rapidly resume full scale underground testing and a substantial nuclear warhead production capacity, computer-integrated with new, high-tech, experimental laboratory facilities. In addition to ensuring the "safety and reliability" of the "enduring" arsenal, Stockpile Stewardship is officially and explicity intended to maintain the capability to design and develop new weapons, and to train a new generation of nuclear weapons designers. Over the next decade, the US plans to invest $45 billion in this programme – an amount, in inflation adjusted dollars, well above the Cold War annual spending average for nuclear weapons research, development, testing and production.

'Stockpile Stewardship will allow nuclear weapons development to continue without full-scale underground tests. Instead, scientists will simulate nuclear tests using the world's fastest supercomputers and data collected from more than 1000 past tests, coupled with new diagnostic information. This information will be obtained from inertial confinement fusion facilities, pulsed power fusion experiments, above-ground hydrodynamic explosions, and subcritical "zero yield" tests conducted deep underground at the Nevada Test Site. These tests involve hundreds of pounds of high explosive material, and up to several pounds of weapon-grade plutonium. They are called 'subcritical" because they do not generate self-sustaining nuclear chain reactions with measurable nuclear yields. The US claims that subcritical tests don't violate the CTB, which does not define a nuclear test. But the CTB obligates the US "not to carry out any nuclear weapon test explosion or any other nuclear explosion". In view of US condemnation of India's and Pakistan's nuclear tests, the subcritical tests, which clearly violate the spirit of the CTB, should be called "hypocritical" tests. Since signing the CTB in September 1996, the US has conducted 6 subcritical tests, the most recent one on February 9th, 1999.

'Some of the key Stockpile Stewardship technologies have been developed as "dual-use" scientific facilities that can be used for both high energy physics research and bomb science. The prime example is the multi-billion dollar, stadium-sized National Ignition Facility (NIF), presently under construction at the Lawrence Livermore National Laboratory in California. The NIF is designed to focus 192 powerful laser beams onto a pea-sized capsule containing deuterium and tritium, forcing the two heavy isotopes of hydrogen to combine through compression, and causing a brief thermonuclear explosion that will create extremely high temperatures approaching those found in full scale underground nuclear tests. If it works, "ignition" will be achieved, producing a self-sustaining fusion reaction. NIF will generate sizeable explosions, central to Stockpile Stewardship. This raises serious questions about whether NIF – and the virtually identical "Project Megajoule", under construction in France, – violates the letter of the CTB . . .'

SUPPORTING IRELAND'S NEUTRALITY

On 25th September 1999, Tony Simpson represented the Russell Foundation at the demonstration in Dublin against Ireland joining Nato's Partnership for Peace.

Irish Prime Minister Bertie Aherne is sweeping Ireland into Nato's nursery organisation with great haste. He is doing this without seeking the views of the people in a referendum on the issue, even though he had previously promised to do so. The Dublin demonstration was called to remind him of his pledge, ahead of the vote in the Dail on entry.

On the day, the traffic halted on O'Connell Street. A huge, green Trojan horse was drawn along at the head of the march. The sound of carnival drums and whistles caught people's attention. At the rally outside the Dail, John Maguire's song 'Bertie, Keep Your Promise' summed up the Taoiseach's dilemma. It's unforgettable refrain, beautifully sung, was:

'It's as plain as a potato
PfP's the same as Nato.'

Tariq Ali rounded off the speeches with a powerful analysis of Nato's expansion, and the growing threats to peace which it poses.

At a meeting of activists after the demonstration, Tony Simpson explained the Russell Foundation's proposal for a European Conference on Peace and Human Rights.

Subsequently, on 9th October, *The Irish Times* published the following letter from the Russell Foundation's Chairman, Ken Coates:

> 'Ireland's example has some influence in other countries. For this reason, it is a pity that the promised referendum on joining Nato's Partnership for Peace has been cancelled. Many people in Eastern Europe are insecure about the possibility that their countries are losing neutrality, and Ireland has always been a beacon for them.
>
> 'We do not agree with Partnership for Peace that peace is a military matter, to be obtained by military means. In the past, we found ourselves in agreement with many Irish people and most Irish politicians on this matter.
>
> 'All these issues need open and democratic discussion. That is why we are preparing to call a European Conference on Peace and Human Rights, where we hope participants from Ireland will play a prominent part.'

An excellent briefing, *The PfP Road from Neutrality to Nato and the WEU*, is available from Peace and Neutrality Alliance (PANA), 113 Springhill Avenue, Blackrock, Co. Dublin, Ireland, e-mail silchester@tinet.ie

HAGUE APPEAL MOVES FORWARD

In May 1999, over 8,000 people gathered for an International Citizens Peace Conference in the Hague.

A representative of the Russell Foundation joined others from a great variety of disarmament, peace, human rights and environmental groups on 4th November, when Bruce Kent convened a follow-up UK meeting in London. Over 50 people crammed into the Friends House committee room, designed to hold only 30.

A lively discussion took place around the 50 proposals on the Hague Agenda, together with the activities and structure planned to further the campaign.

The Hague Agenda for Peace and Justice in the 21st Century emerged from the intensive and widespread consultation during the Hague Appeal for Peace process.

The Agenda reflects the four major strands of the Hague Appeal:

1) Root Causes of War/Culture of Peace;
2) International Humanitarian and Human Rights Law and Institutions;
3) Prevention, Resolution and Transformation of Violent Conflict;
4) Disarmament and Human Security.

Copies of the Agenda can be obtained from the Hague Appeal for Peace 1999, 11 Venetia Road, London N4 1EJ; email: +http://www.haguepeace.org

WAR IN THE BALKANS

Ken Fleet represented the Russell Foundation at the Conference organised by the Birmingham Committee for Peace in the Balkans on 30th October at the University, under the title: 'The Balkans War and NATO's New World Order'. Some 70 people took part.

Canon Paul Oestreicher, Tariq Ali and Misha Gavrilovic of the British-Serbian Peace Alliance opened with useful information about the recent attack by NATO on Yugoslavia, from different perspectives. This plenary was followed by seminars on the character of the war (humanitarian or not?), the media war, and the threats to the environment.

In the afternoon session, Alex Callinicos (York University) argued that the world had become much more dangerous and unstable since the end of the Cold War. There was now no effective opposition to America, the one remaining superpower. Redmond O'Neill (London Committee for Peace in the Balkans) pointed to the widespread increase in poverty and social dislocation which had occured during the last decade. But Gunter Minnerup (Birmingham University) saw hope in the growth of a stronger Europe, on which we might build an alternative platform.

'Although they did not all agree in their analysis of the situation, every speaker recognised that America and NATO represented a very serious threat to peace and human rights, and had to be opposed', said Ken Fleet.

Bruce Kent (Hague Appeal) and Carol Turner (Peace in the Balkans) closed the Conference with accounts of the recent campaigns and appeals to keep up the pressure.

Ken Coates and Tony Simpson spoke at an earlier regional meeting in the same series, in Sheffield, on 9th October, where Alice Mahon MP gave a stirring eywitness account of the deaths, injuries, destruction and environmental damage wrought by the war in Serbia and Kosovo.

Ken Coates raised the issue of the use of depleted uranium in the war against Yugoslavia at a meeting in Athens from 1 to 3rd October. The First Mediterranean Seminar on the Nuclear Threat was convened by the Greek Medical Association for the Protection of the Environment and against Nuclear and Biochemical Threat. It drew wide participation from countries in the region. The next issue of *The Spokesman* will probe the use of depleted uranium in Iraq and Yugoslavia.

A RUSSELL TRIBUNAL ON PSYCHIATRIC TREATMENT

In Hamburg on 6th August 1999, a press conference was called to announce the organisation of a Russell Tribunal on Human Rights in Psychiatry. The Tribunal would address a number of serious concerns about the treatment of those who are deemed to be mentally ill in many Western societies.

The proposed Tribunal would be autonomous and self-sufficient. It will seek to convene its first session in Berlin in the year 2000. The Russell Foundation hopes that all those who are concerned with psychiatric treatment, either as medical practitioners, patients, victims or concerned citizens, will support the Tribunal by offering testimony, whether written or oral, for its consideration.

A Communication

from Mr Jakov Berger

Your collection on the Kosovo tragedy, *Benign Imperialism: The war after the war (Spokesman 65)*, is very much to the point. One issue, however, though touched upon by Dr Zhores Medvedev, requires further comment. It is the cardinal change in the regard for Western 'liberal values' on the part of the Russian liberal intelligentsia, and that of the population generally, before and after the bombing of Kosovo, its occupation, and the whole gamut of naked, imperial ravaging which came to light earlier in 1999, but were, of course, always there.

My point is that the Russians (as well as, among others, the Serbians and others in Yugoslavia) had a sort of quasi-religious outlook on the West as the ideal, a lighthouse to culture and civilisation, as well as being politically a 'Democratic Utopia'. All that might sound like fairy-tale naivety, but it took the unbelievable barbarity of the onslaughts on Kosovo, as well as Iraq, to make possible a rude awakening as to the real nature of that 'civilised society' in the West, in the USA and Western Europe, in England in particular, with the 'iconic' truths from the BBC, and so on.

While Dr Medvedev was writing the observations as published by you (I had an opportunity to read them in Russian beforehand), there was just a time of warning, of apprehension of what might, and would, happen in the world 'after the war'. This war was the first in history to secure a full victory and capitulation just by the sheer scale of inequality between the participants. It was so great that the Yugoslav Army and its Government found themselves in a curious state of paralysis, a moral frustration which was unequalled historically. And this was in the land of the classic Partisan armies, of Tito, of the long struggle against the best forces which Nazi Europe could then gather in the Balkans.

But the most significant after-shock of all that was the reaction of the Russians. They did, after all, find in themselves the unbelievable courage and resources to crush the *Wehrmacht*, the best army ever seen under the sun.

What we now see in Chechnya is quite a different Russia, as the result of recent events, than that which was facing the same terror in 1994, when the internal 'pacifist' forces, those for having 'peace' at any price, were decisive in the humiliation, together with the betrayal on different levels, of course.

But the 'lesson' of Serbia changed everything. While the mortal and military death of the 'smaller Slavic brethren' was depressing, the utter indignation at the wholly unbelievable idea of terrorising the whole country by bombing, by ecocide, by economic demise, followed by occupation, driving away the settled population whom the Turks, Austrians, and Germans could not move though they were defeated – that 'made it'. The the Russians as a nation finally awakened to the West's real values. When they hear appeals from here in Western Europe, and especially from the USA as the leading country in NATO, to go softly on the real terror and the jihad of Basayev's Chechnya – they are a radically changed people from 1989, from 1991, and even from 1996.

Despite the Orwellian 'newsspeak' of the last decade, the change over from socialism to the market, to the 'kleptocracy', was a coup d'etat. It was well rehearsed and effected by Yeltsin and Lebed and some others; a military thing to the core, tanks and 'speznaz' (special forces) and all. Still the intelligentsia, displaying a peculiar Russian trait, saw in the demise of the Bolshevik Revolution a new dawn of utopian peace and harmony. Ploughshares were to replace arms with the 'conversion' of production for military uses. The new peaceful millennium was just round the corner, in place of the strife of Cold War confrontation.

But, after the moral debacle of Kosovo, the realisation could be that the one-power, uni-focal world is even further away from real peace that that of alternative ideas and centres of power. The intelligentsia probably see that the Russians themselves might now lie beneath the enlightened bayonets of the American and British civilising, peace-keeping forces.

They did realise that, after Kosovo. So did the Chinese, who are now putting on display their own missiles which are able to reach targets in the United States. The Chinese are saying, in their own very ancient way, that China will not become a new Indonesia or Taiwan.

Thus, the Kosovo lesson is taken quite universally, I think. That makes your issue on the subject even more important than otherwise.

Reviews

NATO versus Yugoslavia

Peter Gowan, 'The Twisted Road to Kosovo', *Labour Focus on Eastern Europe* **62/1999, £4.00.**

There is an immense reservoir of humane good will in our own country and indeed in most, willing to extend assistance to others in trouble from famine, war or natural disaster. The abuse and manipulation of this honest good will to serve the interests of the powerful is one of the key elements in the governance of affluent democratic states. The two essays in this special issue of *Labour Focus on Eastern Europe* help to strip away the mask of humanitarian rhetoric and allow us a glimpse of the reality of the forces shaping our futures and the lives of millions of people.

The Balkans have always been a crossroads where the dominance of this or that great power has been tested at a dreadful cost in human suffering to the peoples of the region. The last decade has demonstrated once again the appalling cynicism with which such costs are imposed in order to achieve the realpolitik goals of external forces.

The first essay deals with the role of international powers in the dismemberment of Yugoslavia. As Michael Barrett Brown lucidly explained in his book *The Morphology of Debt*, the outbreak of ghastly cycles of violence and atrocity do not take place in isolation. Such outbreaks, as in Rwanda or Colombia, are often eminently predictable and the result of external economic decisions, provoking the collapse of living standards, with the effect of inflaming local social divisions in the scramble for the fast shrinking resources needed to keep communities from destitution.

It is not necessary to look hard to see this process at work in the former Yugoslavia. The strategy of Yugoslav governments in the 1970's, anxious to fund growth through exports by heavy borrowing abroad, hit a brick wall when the Western economies went into recession and closed to Yugoslav exports. The imposition of IMF austerity measures smashed up the system of redistribution that underpinned the Yugoslav political structure and unleashed a process of fragmentation. Far from being countered by the policy of other European states and the Americans, this process was actively encouraged, with the ghastly results of atrocity and civil war, with which we are all familiar. Peter Gowan throws a searchlight on how this was brought about.

The second essay, 'The Euro-Atlantic Origins of NATO's Attack on Yugoslavia,' widens the inquiry to illuminate the construction of the post Cold War world political order. The author argues that the ignition of the Kosovo war was one element in a ten-year campaign by the United States to re-establish its political dominance over the European powers, 'a hegemony whose political basis crumbled with the Berlin wall'. This exercise required the rescue of the NATO and EU projects from the redundancy with which they were faced with the collapse of the Soviet Union.

The successful expansion of NATO to embrace Poland, the Czech Republic and Hungary, combined with a practical military campaign under firm US leadership, has gone a long way towards restructuring and reaffirming a new division of Europe, with the American sphere of influence greatly expanded. Correspondingly, the capacity of an EU, led by a reunited and revivified Germany, to pursue any independent line on the regional or world stage, has been effectively contained. An American led NATO now has the capacity and political legitimacy to intervene beyond its borders behind a highly selectively targeted smokescreen of humanitarian rhetoric to keep the public on side. The Americans have achieved the capacity to impose emergency mobilisations in Europe as and when they need to keep their subordinate powers in order.

These essays are valuable tools for the left in exposing the reality of the policy formation by tiny elites, shaping the contemporary world. These elites speak in coded language before the public. The brutal realities are not to be discussed 'in front of the children'. Those of us with the precious gifts of literacy and access to information have a duty to meet the audacious inversions of reality attempted by the propagandists of the new order head on and point to the policies and programmes which are capable of achieving peace and security for the peoples of Europe and beyond.

David Holland

David Holland is a member of the editorial board of Labour Focus on Eastern Europe, which is available from 30 Bridge St., Oxford, OX2 0BA e-mail HYPERLINK mailto:labfocu@n.apc.org webpage: www.gn.apc.org/labourfocus

Ancient rights

Richard A. Bauman, *Human Rights in Ancient Rome*, Routledge, 1999, xiii & 193pp., £40.00.

Professor Bauman, of the Australian Academy of the Humanities, has written two previous works on aspects of Roman law; here he gives a more general survey of the law as protector of individuals or communities. It is a study at once exciting and very learned; 28 pages of notes to 129 of text may strike a reader as an excessive weight of baggage; but the removal of so much bulk from the text does, as the author says, allow the narrative to move forward with more freedom. It does so chronologically, from the Republican period, starting mainly from the late 3rd century BC, to the Principate, mainly from its setting up by Augustus to 235 AD.

Much philosophical or political thinking of a progressive character went on, under the title of *humanitas*. It was in origin Greek, and Bauman feels that the UNO's 'Declaration of Human Rights' in 1948 differs from it not very much. It is rather, in both cases, a difference of principle from practice that we meet with. Our Declaration forbids torture, but since it was signed torture has gone on spreading far and wide. As Bauman comments, Rome's pious intentions were often frustrated by what was called *utilitas publica*, as our own are liable to be by commercial interests (p.7).

An early chapter is devoted to the Greek background. Most of the civilization of Rome and its Mediterranean empire was derived from Greece, but Greece itself had much to reproach itself with. Bauman cites an essay by the historian Thucydides on the horrifying violence let loose in the 5th Century BC by the outbreak of civil warfare between factions of oligarchs striving to hold on to power, and democrats fighting to dislodge them. 'Human nature, always rebellious, was not quite incapable of controlling itself' (15). Still, it was the Greeks, or some of them, who before long were endeavouring to win acceptance of what they called *philanthropia*, and wanted to see its principles entrenched in law.

Romans were soon separating this general idea into a number of compartments, to give it more distinctness; together they added up to *humanitas*. At their head was *clementia*. We may recall that Mozart wrote an opera about *La Clemenza di Tito*, for an emperor of his own time to listen to and, the composer doubtless hoped, to learn from. Roman thinking stemmed in many ways from the Stoic philosopher Panaetius of Rhodes, who combined his native Greek ethics with Roman realism in a fashion that could appeal to Roman men of action. By virtue of this combination Stoic philosophy was gaining more and more influence. It had few competitors. Rome's official religion was negligible; Platonism was too abstract.

Yet during their conquest of Macedonia, in the later 2nd Century BC, Roman generals were accused of destroying dozens of towns and selling 150,000 of the inhabitants into slavery. There were similar episodes during the Carthaginian wars, which even liberals might defend as necessary in the public interest. Syracuse in Sicily was another victim; and New Carthage in Spain, where the order was given to begin by killing all in sight, and only then turn to plundering.

Cicero was the leading figure of the enlightenment – a middle-class politician on the conservative side, who rose to be consul and fell to being an exile – a brilliant lawyer, a dazzling orator – and the foremost adapter of Greek thought to the Roman mind. Bauman adds that his only contemporary rival in advocating *humanitas* and *clementia* was Caesar (36); an ironical enough tribute, considering Caesar's massacres and sales of prisoners in Gaul. Cicero was a universalist, a champion of the ill-used abroad as well as at home – though not often of slaves. Still, his attitude could at times be distinctly racist, as in the case of the Sardinians; he believed them to be of Carthaginian origin, and that was enough to condemn them. At home he denounced savage modes of punishment like scourging or crucifixion, though he felt able to assert that the worst of such horrors had been abolished long ago. Bauman regards as an important further advance the permission granted to a convicted defendant to avoid the death penalty by going into voluntary exile. It may be asked whether this was much of a boon except to men of means who could take advantage of it. They were not it seems compelled to leave Italy (45).

Chapter 6 examines restraints imposed on oppressors of colonial peoples, in the late years of the Republic. Two chief considerations were at work. One was that arbitrary treatment of provincials, which was all too frequent, would be prejudicial to Rome's reputation for justice, and the prestige this conferred: it was a blot on the *maiestas populi Romani*, the majesty of the Roman people. Most flagrant of many evils was the squeezing of money out of provincials, by governors and their officials, into their own pockets. This habit was scandalously widespread. When J.P. Morgan was taxed with money-grabbing, the great banker is said to have replied: 'I am not in Wall Street for my health.' A Roman governor too often arrived at his post licking his lips, and thinking on very similar lines.

A 'classic example' is that of M. Papillius Laenas, who in 173 BC, after the surrender of a rebel tribe of Ligurians, in north-west Italy, destroyed their town and sold 10,000 people into slavery – a very lucrative line of business (54-5). The Senate took him up sharply, and ordered that the victims be set free and the purchase price restored to the buyers. One doughty champion of human rights in this and other cases was Cato, in most respects a hard man, no sentimentalist but a pillar of everything old and time-honoured. In a case of extortion in Spain, he failed to bring the villain to book, but the prosecution at least 'testifies to the strength of the humanitarian impulse' (56). This showed also in an innovation of that era which allowed the tribunes, as representatives of the people, to prosecute a wrong-doer before the popular assembly, instead of that stronghold of privilege, the Senate.

In spite of this, in 149 BC an orgy of violence in Spain by a governor named Galba went unpunished: he paraded his young children, and the citizens mingled their tears with his own. It was a scene worthy of Hollywood. This was 'the low-water mark' in a long-drawn record of hits and misses (56-7), but it was made up for by the establishment in the same year, thanks to another reformer, Calpurnius Piso, of a permanent jury-court to adjudicate on charges of extortion in the colonies. Cicero was among those who were to preside over it; in this field he was a qualified expert. A series of laws passed in the first six decades of the 1st Century BC further helped to close the doors against the worst barbarities of imperialism.

The triumph in 27 BC of Augustus, the ultimate winner in the contest for power, was 'a watershed in the perception of human rights' (67) – not that he can be supposed to have cared much about them himself, but he must have seen that a firm curbing of lawless excesses would strengthen his prestige and authority. Misrule was restrained more effectively than before. *Humanitas* continued to be the watchword, with *clementia* as a virtue to be extolled in each emperor in turn. Their foremost expounder, perhaps leaving even Cicero behind, was Seneca, the philosophic writer chosen as tutor to the boy Nero, and later killed by him. Nero himself could make a show of disapproval when the murder of an important man by one of his 400 slaves was followed by the customary torture, to extract information, of all the rest, and then their execution (80-1).

Improvements went their difficult way, nonetheless. Castration of slaves was forbidden, child prostitution was at least restricted. There was further legislation against extortion in the provinces. As Bauman points out, this might not be easy to enforce, because of the problem of gathering evidence and witnesses from far away places (87). There were still culprits who indulged their worst instincts with brazen openness. A governor in Asia Minor had 300 people beheaded in a single day, and gloated over the gory spectacle (89-90). One must sometimes wonder whether the powers entrusted to these men (and to many colonial despots of later history) did not go to their heads, infect them with a species of madness. Another sphere of human rights where stalwart champions like the Stoics were needed, was freedom of speech. Its defenders might have to face vigorous repression; this was so especially in the reign of Domitian, a praiseworthy autocrat in some respects, but intolerant of criticism.

Chapter 9 is on 'Man's inhumanity to man'. Sulla's bloodthirsty dictatorship, the proscription-lists of the civil wars, were not repeated under the Principate; but the streak of brutality that helped to make Romans model soldiers persisted. A system of slavery equalled in cruelty only by that of the Christian conquerors of America, helped to nourish it. Seneca was again its most eloquent opponent, but even among Stoics some might be on the wrong side. Torture of free Romans, as well as slaves, seems to have continued all through the Principate. Hadrian forbade any master to kill his slave, or to sell him or her as gladiator or prostitute. But the Arena and its 'Games' survived into the 5th Century, and were only swept away at last by the barbarian invaders (125).

Victor Kiernan

'Present and incorrect'

***Socialist Register, Global Capitalism Versus Democracy*, 1999, edited by Leo Panitch and Colin Leys, Merlin Press, 1999.**

Addressing the Economic Club of Chicago in April 1999, Tony Blair announced that '. . . globalisation is not just an economic, it's also a political and security phenomenon'. Calling for a 'new definition of the international community' the British Prime Minister, Kosovo in mind, noted the West's interest in the 'spread of the value of liberty, the rule of law, human rights, and an open society'. Organising smooth economic development and political freedom are closely linked. The left is told to reform to combine the benefits of globalisation, increases in the world's wealth, through dynamic rivalry, with a grasp of the 'connexity' that demands strengthened international institutions. Addressing a European audience Peter Mandelson, echoing the June joint Blair-Schröder declaration, recommends that socialist and social-democratic governments and parties follow their lead and adapt their strategies to the 'new information age' of 'spectacular technological changes' (*Le Monde*, 23.9.99). For supporters of the Third Way, the economy must become more flexible and dynamic, and the summits of world politics ought to encourage – if need be, as in the Balkans, militarily – the merits of liberal democracy. To labour's modernising internationalists, trade and economic liberalisation, social and political justice, march in tandem.

The *Socialist Register* has long painted a very different picture of globalisation. Writers in this indispensable annual collection have, predominantly, considered that globalisation is an important reality. Objective indicators, of Foreign Direct Investment (FDI), the stretch of financial markets, and the power of Transnational Corporations (TNCs), point towards greater interdependence. However, to editor, Leo Panitch, the nation-state is not contrasted with these movements of world capital, but is seen as a key author of globalisation.[1] The *Register*'s distinctive contribution has been to highlight the links between the liberal domestic policies of today's centre-left, continued international deregulation, growing inequalities and disorder. The apparent loss of sovereignty to institutions such as the World Trade Organisation (WTO) is in reality the international constitutionalisation of liberalism. The basic interests of each separate capitalist state are – perhaps paradoxically – largely retained in this collective structure. At the same time *Socialist Register*'s contributors have opposed the 'progressive competitiveness' economics of the mainstream left. That is, the belief that social values can be furthered within market limits by an educated workforce able to export successfully. Put simply, the case against has been that to work this means playing one country against another, putting social achievements at risk. Third Way attempts to complement this stand with global governance, and extended liberalism, endorse the dominance of whoever emerges as victors.

The 1999 edition of the *Socialist Register, Global Capitalism Versus Democracy*, is published at an important moment. The underside of global economic liberalism and the spread of liberal democratic principles is increasingly visible. The European Social Model is threatened by denationalisation, long-term unemployment and renewed calls for welfare reform and labour flexibility – even in spaces, such as France, where mass opposition seemed to have beaten them off. In New Labour's Britain, and increasingly, other European centre-left governments, social justice, whatever its electoral support, appears a dispensable afterthought to competitiveness. Endorsements of global democratisation, from Anthony Giddens, to the more radical David Held, based on expanded individual autonomy, a varied civil society and multiple sovereignties, are submerged by an inter-state system that gives priority to the interests of secure market societies. The world is now drifting towards cosmopolitan militarism, as the bombing of Yugoslavia is accepted as necessary to squash sovereign states that pose illiberal threats to the West. Part of the left has travelled the same route and now finds itself endorsing what the editors of the *Socialist Register* describe as the 'illusions that have attended capitalism's triumphant march' in a 'vague search for a new international civil society' built up by these institutions (p.vii).

Globalisation as capitalism

The *Socialist Register* concentrates on the political economy of globalisation. In *Capital Vol.1* Marx described the 'entanglement of all peoples in the net of the world market'. Hugo Radice employs these insights to establish that capitalism is intrinsically global. He presents a case against sceptics, Paul Hirst and Grahame Thompson to the fore. These doubters argue that the world economic system underwent a much greater internationalism pre-1914, that the importance of financial trading is exaggerated, that truly global TNCs are rare – the vast majority remaining firmly nationally rooted – and that FDI is limited and restricted to select industrialising countries. In this view states remain free to determine the main areas of policy. Radice musters alternative evidence to suggest that ever deeper world-wide integration cannot be considered as primarily global, and that capital is indeed increasingly fluid, stemming from the exploitative accumulation Marx uncovered. Perhaps Radice's strongest case is made by citing the change-over from Keynesian-welfarist-statist policies to neo-liberal policies. This has been 'so consistent through the past 20 years and all around the world that it is hard to see them as either contingent or the result of independent policy choices by national governments' (p.7). A more inter-dependent world economy, institutions such as the IMF and the World Bank, and neo-liberal states reflect capitalist strength faced with labour's declining market power. This reassertion of corporate and managerial control has brought states into line.

The companion of globalisation in the flesh, is the spiritual ideology of globalisation as the bloom of the best qualities of free-market humus. David Ricardo's eulogy of the 'universal society of nations' brought together by markets, and Adam Smith's system of natural liberty, are welded to information technology. To Radice, if '. . . globalisation is intrinsically a *capitalist* process', it is because it has rewarded capital owners at their workers' expense and everyone's benefit (p.13). From similar premises other contributors investigate the negative effects of international rationalisation and the limits of conventional alternatives. Financial destabilisation in South America and Asia, the ruthless restructuring of American working conditions, and the undermining of European welfare arrangements, are vividly described.

Globalisation's impact on the United Kingdom, and the potential for a return to Keynesian class alliances, are of great importance to British socialists. David Coates demonstrates that Conservative governments accepted that the immediate logic of comparative advantage overrode the country's long-term interest in manufacturing. Now, in the UK, a growth strategy based on financial services, 'low wages and intensified work routines' and weak unions, has ensued, though not without a cheap cost niche on the world bazaar. The Swedish model of high salaries, security and solid unions, is less acceptable in the same environment. Its domestic capitalists have faced international competition, and, with the ability to shift capital off-shore, have fewer ties to their home country and less obligation to sustain the class compromise that sustained this settlement. To Coates neo-liberalism cannot deliver equalitarian standards of living. But neither can Swedish style 'national-class compacts' be recreated which 'allow wages and profits to rise together in core capitalist economies' (p.136). Coates' assumption, more explicit than that of others, is that capital is more powerful 'ostensibly because capital is more globally mobile, actually, because of the steady proletarianisation of the Asian peasantries' (*ibid*). We are left to conclude that New Labour is either unable or unwilling to abandon the advantages of a low-wage economy and undertake a shift in competitiveness policy that Coates, in contrast to the *Register*'s editors, has previously claimed may progressively develop manufacturing and radical social reform.

The state plays a central role in many of these transformations. To Konstantinos Tsoukalas we are entering a new phase of imperialism. There is no longer a 'geographical partition of the globe into more or less defined zones of imperialist influence and dominance'. Instead 'Direct exploitation of labour can be pursued by capitalists in various social formations simultaneously . . .' (p.57). Tsoukalas' principal insight is that the national bourgeoisie has been replaced with what the left-wing Eurocommunist state theorist Nicos Poulanztas called the 'interior bourgeoisie' ensconced in a neo-liberal state. In somewhat dense paragraphs it emerges that the state now carries out the deregulation process because it reproduces the transterritorial mobility of capital and its strategies of accumulation. Government bureaucracies are increasingly tied to the private sector. We might conjuncture that the spread into Europe of pro-business state and parties on the US pattern indeed confirm Poulantzas' claim that there would be duplication of 'the form of the dominant imperialist power within each national formation and its state'.[2]

A landscape emerges of a global liberalised economy exploiting all the available possibilities to maintain profit levels, regardless of the consequences for the world's population. The stock-exchange ticker-tape that rules the freedom of the media in the film *Network* (1976) is updated and computerised. The *Socialist Register* nevertheless, has little discussion of the mechanisms behind the process. Marx asserted that capital would expand its operations to any state function if a sufficient rate of return was available. Recent literature suggests a destructive spiral of horizontal competition between capitalists stemming from unresolved over-accumulation (Robert Brenner), or the rise of a network-society in which the world of financial 'flows' moulds and fragments societies (Manuel Castells). More politically Giovanni Arrighi has argued that American hegemony is dissolving in a cyclical phase of financial liquidity, and that, amongst other possibilities, it may use its state and war-making capacity to retain dominance through a 'truly global empire'.[3] In these accounts, and others, the rule of number-crunchers over welfare and the working class stems from far-reaching dynamics. Attempts to control democratically the economy face more profound structural obstacles than pro-market governments of the centre-left, neo-liberal states, and corporate decision-makers.

Strategic alternatives

The view that the state is a central actor in globalisation is both paralysing and emancipating. Anxious to deny it a potentially autonomous decision-making, yet keen to imply cabinets, ministries and bureaucracies, in market expansion, the state's actors are regarded as agreeing to a weakened sovereignty, and to retrenchment around liberalism. The problem for those who want to liberate democratic political energy is to disentangle objective constraints from self-binding limitations. The *Socialist Register* leans towards a straightforward assault on the external limits. Joachim Hirsch calls for an 'emancipatory democratic social movement' organised with a 'new internationalism' (p.288). Unfortunately, examples of such movements, such as the Liverpool dockers and defence of the Renault Vilvoorde car plant, ran up against the superior power of capital. Vilvoorde revealed the difficulties of a French Socialist government shareholder which feared the effects of a resistance to closure on its own inward investors. Apart from Coates, few of the contributors appear willing to engage seriously with the social democratic parties bound to negotiate with globalisation by virtue of their political power. It is difficult, of course, to imagine that they need to stuff their ears with wax in order to be deaf to the sirens of radical socialism. Yet it is surely an important task, while we wait for Hirsch's 'anti-capitalist revolution'.

Boris Kagarlitsky illustrates firmly the terrain where the left has to fight. The left must use the 'state as a bridgehead in the struggle for real power' (p.294). If new institutions are required to take apart the ties with domestic and international capital, then now would be a good time to propose them. Whatever the boundaries of its power, the position of the state is examined all the way down. Constitutional reform, which some of the *Register*'s contributors saw as a step towards the democratic transformation of the British state, even its economy, is underway, though not perhaps, to challenge global pressures. The air is full of the sound of those, including some on the left, proposing a cosmopolitan liberal militarism, buttressed by autonomous civil society, and founded on a universal law and markets that override national sovereignty. An alternative internationalist civil society, despite its vagueness, has shown signs of life. The workers movement and radical forces have benefited from improved global communications, not least in proliferating Web sites, which are seed-beds for informed internationalism. If the *Socialist Register* has only begun to open up some of the issues posed by globalisation, socialism and democracy, it perhaps reflects the emerging and still unsure state of the democratic, socialist wave of globalisation.

Andrew Coates

References

1. Leo Panitch, *Rethinking the Role of the State*, James H. Mittelman (Editor). *Globalisation: Critical Reflections*, Lynne Rienner, Colorado/London, 1997.
2. Nicos Poulantzas, *Classes in Contemporary Capitalism*, p.73, Verso, London, 1978.
3. Giovanni Arrighi, *The Long Twentieth Century*, p.355, Verso, London, 1994.

Capitalism in crisis

Young Person's Guide to the Global Crisis, and the Alternative by **Michael Barratt Brown (Spokesman 1999) (£9).**
The May Day Manifesto, Part One, Defending the Welfare State by **Michael Barratt Brown (Spokesman 1998) (£6.99).**

New Labour politicians, academics and the media dismiss traditional Labour policies and socialist ideas as outdated. The problems we face today in a globalised world economy are totally different from those of the past, they argue.

Michael Barratt Brown in his *Young Person's Guide to the Global Crisis* has provided an expert, but clear, analysis of the problems of globalism and the sort of policies required to tackle them, which fundamentally challenges the New Labour argument. It is succinct – little over a hundred pages long – and costs under £10. As such, it should be read by all who seriously wish to understand the nature of the economic crisis of the contemporary world system – not just by youth, to whom it is particularly addressed.

In the course of his exposition, the author explains how the economic policies widely adopted in many countries at the end of the Second World War in 1945 produced high growth rates, and increasing prosperity for a quarter of a century. These were essentially based on the ideas of the economist John Maynard Keynes, and involved high levels of government expenditure, increased taxation of the wealthy, full employment and the building of the welfare services.

He goes on to explain that this period was brought to an end by a crisis linked to large US current account deficits, which led to the creation of the Euro-dollar market, the abandonment of vital features of the postwar Bretton Woods financial settlement, and the high jump in oil prices from $1.30 per barrel in the 1960s, to $15 in 1977, with the tripling of prices in 1973. At root, however, he suggests it was a crisis of over-production, resulting essentially in the workforce being unable to buy back all the products of their work.

High government expenditures and the efforts of trade unions to push up wages at a time of rising prices were, however, blamed, and monetarist economic theories, in favour of reducing public expenditure and freeing market forces from intervention and regulation, received a gigantic boost. They triumphed fully with the advent to power of Margaret Thatcher and Ronald Reagan.

Michael Barratt Brown, however, shows how economic growth rates slumped, and never recovered up to the present time. In this environment, multinational companies grew, and in 1997, 350 of them accounted for 40% of global trade. Far from this providing for the determination of prices by competition, most are fixed in transfer pricing agreements between their branches. Governments dare not interfere or impose heavy taxes on profits in case investments are switched out of their countries, causing heavy losses of jobs and income. Liberalisation of trade, deregulation, the functioning of the World Trade Organisation, and – if it eventually comes about – the Multilateral Agreement on Investment, increasingly enable giant corporations to make decisions which were previously within the province of the governments of national states. As a result, boosting profits takes priority over citizens' needs.

The author quotes numerous authorities to show how ownership of wealth has been increasingly concentrated in fewer and fewer hands, while poverty has gone up by leaps and bounds. The richest countries now account for 86% of all consumption, and the poorest for just 1.3%. However, within the richest – above all, the USA – there is vast poverty and deprivation.

The book carefully explains how the 1997 crisis in Eastern Asia came about, with the collapse of financial institutions, and spread to Russia and Latin America. It shows how insistence by the IMF on opening up the Russian economy and financial liberalisation deprived the Russian authorities of the means of preventing theft and fraud by robber capitalists, or of compelling them to pay taxes.

The threat of a more far-reaching crisis which could engulf us all has not, however, gone away.

New Labour's ideas of making people more employable and labour more flexible does not touch the root of the problem. The author contends that income has to be redistributed from rich savers to poor spenders, and governments have to be prepared to intervene to create jobs. This will not, however, work for single countries acting alone, but requires common action by countries acting together. He quotes the former 'Delors Plan' for creating 15 million new jobs in the European Union as an example of what might have been done.

Defending the welfare state is touched on within this study, but is dealt with much more fully in *The May Day Manifesto*, originally published for May Day 1998, but still very pertinent to the situation today.

The manner in which the former Conservative Government attacked the welfare state is covered, and the resulting reduction in social security provision from one of the best to one of the worst in Europe.

Unfortunately, however, the Blair Government from the outset accepted that further 'reform' of the welfare system was vital in order to reduce costs. This explains its policy of seeking to encourage people to come off welfare, to work, its rejection of the principle of universal benefits in favour of targetting and means tests, its refusal to restore the link between pension and earnings, and the massive reduction planned in disability benefits payments, etc.

Michael Barratt Brown refutes the justification advanced for these and other steps designed to cut back welfare, and sets out an alternative strategy.

At a time when there is growing unease within the Labour and Trade Union movements about the direction which the present government is taking - and this is beginning to be reflected in widespread abstentions in elections - it is vital to understand the problems clearly, and to recognise that the socialist alternative and traditional Labour values have not been rendered obsolete, but are still fully valid.

These two books provide an excellent exposition of this position, and totally refute the ideas on which New Labour seeks to base its case. Sooner or later these will be swept away, anyway, by the course of events. Those who wish to understand why, and to work for the ultimate victory of the true Labour cause, need to read both these books.

Stan Newens

Smells from Spooks' Corner

Christopher Andrew and Vasili Mitrokhin, *The Mitrokhin Archive: The KGB in Europe and the West*, Allen Lane, The Penguin Press, 996pp., £25.

Vasili Mitrokhin laboured in the KGB archives for years, bundling up the papers for their move to better quarters outside Moscow. He worked assiduously, and was commended for his efforts. But all the time he was copying highly classified papers longhand, and smuggling them out of the archives. In 1992 it became time to go, and Mitrokhin was smuggled out by the British Secret Service, together with his massive collection of notes.

British Intelligence called in Christopher Andrew to edit these papers, in close co-operation with Mitrokhin himself. The result is this very dense volume of almost a thousand pages, which has already been extensively drawn upon throughout the Western press.

Of course the book is full of names, and has exposed a number of spies whose efforts had hitherto been unremarked. This part of its revelations has been widely reported. Less widely appreciated has been the fact that Soviet Intelligence specialised in two kinds of information. Yes, of course there was straightforward espionage, which, for instance, was considerably preoccupied with the recipe for hydrogen bombs. But a prodigious amount of effort was also invested in enquiries into the activities of rival political groups, usually involving dissident socialists of one kind or another.

Early on we learn of the obsessional preoccupation with Trotsky and his followers. Trotsky's son became the target for a NKVD agent, Mark Zborowski, who was so profoundly trusted that he was given the key to the letterbox and entrusted with Trotsky's most confidential file and archives. Mitrokhin chronicles the surveillance and destabilisation of various groups of Trotskyists. Various murders were committed. Burglars were commissioned to steal Trotsky's papers, an exercise which was somewhat otiose, since Zborowski was already the custodian of the main archive, now located at Harvard. But the obsession with Trotsky, culminating in his assassination, kept a large number of KGB residents very busy, and confirmed some very bad habits which persisted long after 1940, when the Communist leader was murdered in Mexico.

Later, the socialist opposition having been very largely liquidated, the post-Stalin KGB found itself deployed in an extensive series of efforts against the dissidents, beginning with Abram Tertz, Sinyavsky and Daniel, and progressing to Solzhenitsyn and Sakharov.

Mitrokhin's notes cover the 1973 trial of Yakir and Krasin, who were among the co-founders of the Samizdat journal, *Chronicle of Current Events*.

Yakir was the son of a general who had been put to death after the Moscow trials. He was induced to confess, and recant. Later, Krasin, too, broke. The KGB had a great deal of work to do in assisting these confessions. The whole process culminated in a KGB press conference in which both Yakir and Krasin 'paraded their guilt and remorse'.

The production of this book raises many interesting questions about the conduct of the Western Intelligence Services, and the means by which Mitrokhin's secret notes have been deployed in one country after another, usually to benefit the right.

Of course, these papers might tell us a lot, if they were accessible in undiluted form. But having been carefully edited, there is some reason to be suspicious about their use in current political arguments. That the KGB was an instrument of reaction is beyond reasonable doubt. But an enemy of my enemy is not necessarily my friend, and the Western Intelligence Services, even in democratic countries, seem to share all too many characteristics with their Soviet adversary.

James Smith

Horace and the Middle Way

Horace: Poetics and Politics, **V.G. Kiernan, St. Martins Press, 204pp.**

Those who have known Victor Kiernan over the years have been aware of his habit of carrying a volume of the writings of the Latin poet Horace in his pocket. We have been promised that one day we should be able to enjoy the fruits of his readings in a celebratory volume. Thanks, he says, to the 'inestimable' 'help and encouragement' of his wife Heather, we now have this brilliant new book from Victor in his 80s. It is a must for anyone who wishes to get the feel of Latin poetry in the Augustan age – that of Virgil, Horace, Ovid, – and to understand the politics of the long 40 years rule of Augustus. And it has lessons for our own times, two millennia later.

The Augustan Age of the Restoration and of early Eighteenth Century English poets and writers – Pope and Dryden, Swift and Dr Johnson – was so-called after the rule of the first Roman Emperor, Caesar's great nephew, who was given the title Augustus. That the two ages were thus compared was for two reasons: in both a long period of relative peace followed a century of civil war; in both, and by the same token, writers felt constrained and enabled to refine their sense and their style. Moderation and common sense replaced the extremes of argument and ideology. A middle way or golden mean was the aspiration of every philosopher.

In both these ages the peace was relative. The Treaty of Utrecht of 1713, ending war with France and Spain, gave Britain most of Canada and control of the slave trade, and in the next forty years Gibraltar, Georgia (North America) and Bengal were all added to the British Empire. Augustus made peace with the Parthians, but by his defeat of Antony and Cleopatra, the whole Mediterranean basin and Europe north and west of the Rhine, modern Turkey, Syria and Judaea were held within the Roman Empire by the force of the imperial legions. Most of these were made up of non-Romans, just like the Indians in the Nineteenth Century British Indian Army and the Gurkhas in the British forces in Kosovo today. Rome under Augustus was based on slavery, which was accepted as perfectly natural. Kiernan comments that this would have drawn no more comment than the relation of labour to capital in our society today.

Quintus Horatius Flaccus (Horace as we call him, but do not call Lucretius Lucrece or Epicurus Epicure) was the son of a freed slave. He retained for much of his life a chip on the shoulder, as we would say, for this fact, although he became in the event the Emperor's poet laureate. His father paid for him to go to Athens for his education, which determined the classical style of his poetry. As a young man he there became a senior officer under Brutus on the side of the republicans and subsequently made jokes about having run away when Brutus was defeated by Octavian at Philippi in 42 BC. After that he had to make his way cautiously back into favour when Octavian became the emperor Augustus. While he established himself as a writer, he was always critical of corruption and of the over-indulgence of the rich elite, but he was fundamentally a trimmer, first as the protégé of his wealthy protector Maecenas and later as the Emperor's own poet.

Horace's first work, the satires, are not satirical in our sense. They are rather moralising chats, with roots in the countryside outside Rome, where Maecenas had got for him a small villa and some land. Despite his father's origins Horace had no qualms about employing slaves to work the land and care for him, although friends laughed at his occasionally wielding the hoe himself and joining in the seasonal labours. Many of the slaves would not even be local people; these would have migrated to the towns and particularly to Rome to enjoy a parasitic life of 'bread and circuses'. While huge resources were devoted to maintaining the empire and 'a few plutocrats with platoons of slaves', a farm within 30 miles of Rome, Kiernan points out, would be in 'a backward region, afflicted with bad roads, bad food and water, bad inns'. Rome was for Horace as for Virgil an idealised concept. Horace's belief in a golden mean would have made him, as Kiernan puts it 'a natural partisan of a genuine middle class, if he could have found one. But he was left stranded between corrupt aristocracy and degenerate mob.'

The Epodes which link the Satires and the Odes reveal a dark side of Horace's life written in the last stages of the civil war. Horace fears that Rome will be overwhelmed by barbarians, and cannot conceal from himself that this may be deserved. Alongside this he shows his fear of witches, of sudden death and of the spells that women can weave. Horace was never married and his amatory poems addressed to both men and women have no passion and do not carry conviction. Only wine, which appears again and again as his solace, will free men's hearts from dire disquiets. Although he was described contemporaneously as pot-bellied, Horace wrote abstemiously about food, enjoying in his own home a simple vegetarian diet.

The Odes are Horace's master work, the first three books published in about BC 23, when the poet was 40 and Augustus's rule was in its third year. Kiernan points out that the Ode was in Latin *carmen*, origin of our charm or spell; it was designed to be sung or recited with a musical accompaniment. Lyric poetry is so called because originally written for the lyre. It is a very personal expression, although the subject matter may be public. In Horace the metre is strict, based on the Greek, although the sense flows on from stanza to stanza and from theme to theme. I can myself recall the pleasure as a schoolboy of fitting those great Latin polysyllables – *incomparabilis, inexorabilis, illacrimabilis* – into the metric grid and ending the lines with a monosyllabic thump, emulating Horaces's famous

'*Parturient montes, nascetur ridiculus mus*'.

Much of the material of the Odes goes beyond the limits of rational thought and derives from mythology and especially, as Kiernan emphasises, 'from the bardic epics, the Iliad and Odyssey, which went under the name of Homer.' There is a private voice in the Odes, with which Horace speaks of his farm and the Sabine countryside, his hopes and his fears, especially of death, insomnia and his chronic hypochondria, his 'Byronic gloom', sometimes also of his loves and pleasures. This is all mixed up with reference to the Gods of ancient Greek mythology, not in a religious sense, for Horace was not religious. He was not even a Stoic. He believed with Zeno in following the path of virtue, but this should not include self-denial; he liked his wine too much for that. *Carpe diem*! Seize the day! *Eheu fugaces*! The fleeting years slip by. *But Nil desperandum*! Never despair! It is the cry of all the great lyric poets through the centuries, but with Horace there is a magnificent human fortitude unbuttressed by any spiritual faith – he who said '*Non omnis moriar*', I shall not altogether die.

The public voice of the Italian patriot in the Odes is, however, the stronger one, and in this too Horace calls on the Gods, but rather to provide allegories for his political comment than to appeal to supra-natural forces. The role of the poet laureate is a difficult one, especially in times of change. The present English incumbent has emphasised the need to remain your own man (there have so far been no women, though one would have been a popular choice this time). Horace certainly did that. An official poet must respond to important public events and if his mode is lyrical, his personal involvement cannot be avoided. This was not easy for Horace. He came reluctantly to accept the benefits of a principate in place of the old republic. He despised and reviled the fat cats – the traffickers and usurers, who moved in to take the place of the old aristocracy (we can sympathise today!), but he feared, even hated, the common herd, that fickle multitude (*vulgus infidum*).

What then did Horace have to say to his contemporaries? In the light of his love of the peaceful countryside and warnings against the individual excesses of the Roman generals' plunder of the whole world, it seems disappointing to Kiernan, as it must to us all, that Horace should heap such lavish praise upon the rugged, fighting spirit of the Roman soldier and extol the subjugation of 'barbarian' peoples to Roman law. Of course, he was writing as the official poet to celebrate the victories of Roman arms, but his most famous adage, taken from the Spartan poet Tyrtaeus, *'Dulce et decorum est pro patria mori'*, sweet and fitting is it to die for one's country, is just 'The Old Lie', as Wilfred Owen dubbed it. Horace prefers to take his examples of heroic feats of arms from earlier wars, notably those against Carthage, when Rome was so nearly defeated by Hannibal's African armies and further back still from the Trojan War, although he writes also of this to a friend as 'senseless folly'. As Kiernan shows, Horace is full of contradictions. Wars are *matribus detestata*, but they end with the blessings of peace and the 'wide-stretching majesty of empire' (*imperi porrecta maiestas*). 'Order has been established, crime checked, prosperity restored to the countryside', although Horace knew only too well that it was not like that at all. We too know this very well today, as we are regaled by the Government spin doctors. There is no evidence of sudden prosperity during the reign of Augustus.

In his old age (his death at 57 was the norm for his times; Augustus's 70 years were exceptional) Horace turned to writing Epistles, letters in verse. Most are letters to real people. All are written to men, none to women. They are introspective and often retrospective. Kiernan quotes Hugh Barrow claiming Horace as the first autobiographer. One of the epistles has been singled out by subsequent critics as an essay on The Art of Poetry, much of it concerned with the nature and history of drama, which Horace himself never attempted. It contains the famous 'A poem is like a painting', to which William Temple added 'and rhyme is like the frame', and the complaint that 'sometimes even the good Homer nods.' But the main thrust of the epistles is moral guidance of a peculiarly negative sort, what should not be done. 'Nothing too much' as inscribed on the temple of Apollo at Delphi was no doubt the source of Horace's *Nil admirari*, don't be carried away. His recommended *aequus animus*, which he associates with the Golden Mean, is not just our 'equanimity', for the mean is *mediocritas*, not at all our mediocrity, but a position equally removed from two opposite and unsatisfactory extremes.

Kiernan complains that this avoidance of evil gives no indication of what should be done, even on a personal level of self improvement, let alone envisaging social change. Virtue is its own reward, but how to achieve it is left to each of us to find our own way. Horace does recognise that his freedom is more important to him than the protection of his patron, which he would sacrifice if his freedom were to be impugned. He understands that he is exceptionally fortunate, threatened as he is all round by insecurity, injustice, violence and death in most brutal ways. His highest hope is to be at peace with himself, but the decay of old institutions had left him very much alone.

Kiernan sees Horace's search for a tranquillity and self control, that he never found, as suggesting a 'Hindu or Buddhist atmosphere rather than anything "European"', and how many of Horace's fellow human beings could enjoy his life of gentlemanly leisure for contemplation? Horace could not believe in any of the new ideas of a redeemer and an 'after-life' that were filtering into Rome from the East in his day. So the middle way turns out not to be so golden after all. Without the building of new institutions and a commitment of men and women to social change, a middle way which seeks only to avoid the extremes of personal power and state power leads back once more to the slavery from which we came.

Michael Barratt Brown

Is Ireland still neutral?

John Maguire, *Defending Peace: For an alternative to NATO/PfP and a militarised Europe*, Vote First/Afri, 1999, Irish £2.50 from Afri (Action from Ireland), Grand Canal House, Lr. Rathmines Road, Dublin 6. Also available through the Internet at http://migration.ucc.ie/defendpeace.htm

The North Atlantic Treaty Organisation's expansion continues apace, East and West.

Far to the East, closer to the Indian than the Atlantic Ocean, and right on Russia's doorstep in the Southern Caucasus, Georgia's President Eduard Shevardnadze recently stated his intention to 'knock loudly on Nato's door'. He seeks membership for his troubled state 'within five years'. Whether his hopes will be realised in this highly volatile region remains far from certain. Certainly, the Russians do not look kindly on Nato's encroachments on their borders.

Yet, at the same time, and far more quickly, another strategic addition to Nato's cohort is being engineered. This time it is at the far western end of the Eurasian landmass, right on the North Atlantic itself. Ireland is to join Nato's soothingly, but misleadingly, named 'Partnership for Peace'.

Thus, if Nato's planners have their way, the last neutral voices in western Europe are to be swept away. They will be walled up in the new 'security architecture' which is to lock up the continent, and possibly much of the wider world. For Ireland follows neutral Austria, Finland, Sweden and Switzerland into this alleged 'Partnership for Peace'.

It is always as well to be wary, as Frank Blackaby has warned, when military organisations adopt the word 'peace'. The US Strategic Air Command had as its motto 'peace is our profession' at a time when it was sending B52s with nuclear bombs to loiter near the Soviet border. President Reagan decided to christen the MX Intercontinental Ballistic Missile the 'Peacekeeper'.

'Partnership for Peace' programmes might suggest such items as educational programmes in schools designed to encourage children not to hate other nationalities, or the financing of films which show the appalling consequences of modern war. In fact, the Nato Partnership for Peace programmes are concerned exclusively with the military: peace is a military matter, to be obtained by military means. So PfP programmes involve such items as joint military exercises, force planning and the development of inter-operability between armed services.

Thus, in March 1999, PfP members Poland, the Czech Republic and Hungary were all absorbed into Nato's integrated military command. The military fault line in Europe moved hundreds of kilometres to the East, closer to Russia's borders. How, then, might we yet thwart Nato's ambitions to absorb Ireland?

John Maguire's informative booklet is a good place to start. It gives a clear insight into a crucial strand of the resistance to this surrender of Ireland's active neutrality, and its wider implications. His purpose is

> 'to convince my fellow citizens that we should oppose the creation of a militarised Europe. This would involve not joining NATO's so-called "Partnership for Peace", and also seriously questioning the current direction of the European Union in foreign policy, defence and security. The first step in this questioning is to hold the current Government to the Taoiseach's promise of a consultative referendum on entry to NATO/PfP'.

And a convincing case it is. All the more so because the Irish Government has performed a total u-turn on the issue. In 1997, the governing party, Fianna Fail, stated in its election manifesto: 'We oppose Irish participation in Nato itself, in Nato led organisations such as Partnership for Peace, or in the Western European Union beyond observer status'. Mr Aherne, the party leader and Taoiseach, had told the Irish parliament, the Dail, that joining PfP without a referendum would be 'fundamentally undemocratic'. It had been suggested that such a referendum might have been held on the same day as the European elections, in June this year.

In the event, the Government had second thoughts. One can only surmise that they expected to lose. For Ireland's neutrality is held in high regard in many sections of the community. And the argument that joining PfP is some how the duty of 'good Europeans' seems to cut little ice outside the opinion columns of parts of the Irish press.

Indeed, there have been many complaints that the public debate about this major change in Ireland's status was widely suppressed in the Irish media. Such suppression is a great pity. *The Irish Times*, among others, is usually refreshingly open by comparison to the London media. Now, with the advent of PfP, we read of Ireland's plans to purchase fighter-bomber aircraft and new military vehicles. Free and open discussion is undermined, as this unpopular commitment has been bulldozed through.

At the same time, Nato has gone to war against Yugoslavia. Mr Maguire sets out to learn the lessons of Kosovo. He examines the war

> 'as an example of the kind of military action regarded as both justified and successful by those who want us to move closer to Nato and/or to integrate ourselves into an evolving "European defence identity".'

His conclusion is very clear.

'Nato has done what it did because it was able to do so, without trying to convince others, still less the UN as such, that it was entitled to. This is a ghastly departure in the "post-Cold War" era, ensuring the continued equation of right with might and clearly "marking the card" of any other would-be power bloc. This is no idle projection about the future; the current situation in Dagestan, for example, not only is alarming in itself but has all the potential volatility of a Slavic/Islamic confrontation.'

What would John Maguire have Ireland do instead? He is a critical champion of the United Nations Organisation. Writing on the day when the UN's withdrawal from East Timor had been announced, and then postponed for 24 hours, he says:

'For some, this day puts an end to any hope of the UN's playing a morally and practically adequate role in crises. Though fully respecting that sad conclusion, I do not share it. I still hope that we will learn Erskine Childers' lesson that the UN itself has been held hostage to the rich nations' club; to write it off now would be to legitimise the lawless, aggressive militarism of that same club'.

It is much to be hoped that John Maguire will continue to develop this discussion. As the true picture of Nato's expansion unfolds in the brave new world after the war against Yugoslavia, it is people power and impassioned critical analysis such as this which will help to defend peace and human rights against the new militarism which threatens the world.

Tony Simpson

Disarmament – progress and backsliding

SIPRI Yearbook 1999. Armaments, Disarmament and International Security,
Oxford University Press, 1999, 772pp.

The Stockholm International Peace Research Institute is still beavering away, although the cold war has come and gone, and the arms race has mutated into a confusion of races, including those which depend on recycling rusty, second-hand weapons. SIPRI follows the fragmentation closely, and has produced the common man's guide to the armed collisions which are concluding the present century, and setting their mark on the opening of the next millennium.

In 1998 there were twenty-seven major armed conflicts in twenty-six locations throughout the world. Two involved different States: one between India and Pakistan, and the other between Eritrea and Ethiopia. Six new conflicts erupted during that year: one in Europe and five in Africa. These last involved continuing struggles in Angola, Ethiopia and Eritrea, and the Democratic Republic of Congo. Rwanda and the Congo generated horrific new dimensions of violence. In Europe, the Kosovo Liberation Army had announced a guerrilla campaign in November 1997, and became locked in combat from February 1998. Asia continued to generate many conflicts, and wider turbulence was reflected in the detonation of a nuclear explosion in Pakistan.

The region of the Caspian Sea is boiling with turmoil, as the problem of oil transportation passing through neighbouring territories becomes increasingly pressing.

In some areas, notably Northern Ireland, conflict has died back. But the underlying trends are not encouraging, because 'the general decline in arms production has ceased'. The top one hundred companies involved in the business generated arms sales of $156 billion in 1997. Russian arms production had declined to ten per cent of the late cold war levels, but during 1998 had began to grow again, by five per cent in real terms.

In Europe there is a contradictory progress. The approval of a Code of Conduct for arms exports could be very important, if it were to be more widely extended. But Europeans have come under the closer influence of the United States, particularly during the Nato bombardment of Yugoslavia. Now, the argument is about whether European States will seek military autonomy, or whether they will try to integrate their armaments with those of the Americans, who are certainly greatly advantaged by the state of their technology, and the critical mass of their military industry.

SIPRI have commissioned careful studies of conflict zones, in Africa, in Kashmir, and of course in Kosovo. They treat on the situation in Tajikistan, the Caspian Basin and the Caucasus, and the Middle East. They examine the military reforms in Russia, and the challenges of European defence and security policy. There is a learned paper on military expenditure in China.

The usual summaries of developments on arms control and disarmament agreements are included, as is a worthwhile chronology.

Struggling with all this evidence, SIPRI established an independent working group back in 1996. The report of this group sought to establish a right of co-operative intervention under the Authority of the UN Security Council. But there is still an impasse in the UN, because no-one has found how to square the commitments of the Universal Declaration of Human Rights with the foundation of the UN Organisation on the recognition of national sovereignty. The Stockholm researchers can give us a mine of information about the nature of this impasse, and its many complications: but they are no further forward than the rest of us in prescribing a workable solution.

Ken Coates